OUR PAST BEFORE US
WHY DO WE SAVE IT?

*

Edited by
DAVID LOWENTHAL
and
MARCUS BINNEY

TEMPLE SMITH · LONDON

First published in Great Britain 1981

Maurice Temple Smith Limited
Gloucester Mansions
Cambridge Circus
London WC2

ISBN 0 85117 219 9

Printed and bound in Great Britain by
The Blackwell Press

OUR PAST BEFORE US

Contents

List of Illustrations

Credits for Illustrations

1-4, Peter MacKarell; 5-7, Randolph Langenbach; 8, Roy Westlake; 9, Sylvia Sayer; 12, Christopher Dalton; 14-17, English Tourist Board; 18, 19, 24, 28, 30, David Lowenthal; 20, 21, 23, Marcus Binney; 22, 25, Charles Jencks (*Bizarre Architecture*, London, Academy Editions, 1979); 26, George Rollie Adams; 27, Ralph J. Christian; 29, Venturi, Rauch and Scott Brown; 31, Hazel Cook, Architectural Association.

Introduction

DAVID LOWENTHAL

SAVING HISTORIC sites and objects has become a widely popular cause. Although pollution, neglect, and the bulldozer still take a heavy toll, more and more is now being rescued. The growth of the preservation movement is one of the major social phenomena of our time. It has brought together all manner of people in a common purpose – the recording and saving of their heritage. And it has already profoundly affected the shape and contents of the world around us.

But those who advocate saving things seldom stand back to examine the larger meaning of their enterprise. Why does it matter to preserve buildings, artifacts, and landscapes from previous epochs? What does our tangible heritage signify to us as individuals, as communities, and as nations? How can we make best use of what we succeed in keeping from the tooth of time? And how can we avoid debasing such relics in the process of suiting them to our aims?

To examine these questions the editors of this volume convened a symposium in London in 1979. Fifteen invited speakers and 150 other participants discussed the sources of historic preservation, its implications for our sense of our heritage and of ourselves, and its consequences for the future. All the authors have revised their original contributions, bringing fresh insights and material to this book. Each essay retains its own perspective and flavour, but the editors have recast them into a coherent framework highlighting four emergent themes: the growth and shape of the preservation movement; the range of preservation concerns; varieties of community problems and responses; and how to cope with the increasing popularity of historic places and artifacts.

Introduction

No other study comparable to this one exists. As a self-conscious movement, preservation is still too new to have attracted much critical analysis. Though several books narrate the progress of preservation – notably the conservation of buildings – in particular countries, no general history of the subject has appeared. Little is known of the philosophy or psychology of preservation. This book does not fill these gaps, but at least points the way towards the larger issues that preservation raises – issues which must ultimately be faced to set future priorities for dealing with the legacy of the past.

Why preservation has become so popular an activity is little understood. Remnants of our past lie all around us, some whole, some decayed, some in shreds and tatters, some to be discerned only in traces. Throughout most of history men have mainly ignored these vestiges. Taking their inheritance pretty much for granted, they have allowed relics of antiquity to survive, to decay, or to vanish, according to the whims of nature and of their fellow men.

Isolated instances of deliberate preservation can be cited from time immemorial, to be sure, and certain relics are traditionally treasured – the memories of great men, for example, and their interred or mummified remains. But to retain any substantial part of the material works of our predecessors is an idea of quite recent vintage. Renaissance humanists often mourned the loss of classical antiquities, yet not until Raphael did anyone seek to prevent their continual extinction. Recent centuries, especially the past hundred years, have witnessed a concerted effort to keep such vestiges and preserve them from further decay and destruction. And today virtually every modern state feels some obligation to safeguard historic monuments from vandalism, neglect, and redevelopment.

At the heart of historic preservation lies the view that the tangible past is attractive or desirable. This view is initially rooted in the Renaissance perception of a classical antiquity sharply distinguishable from, and superior to, the recent past. The new appreciation of classical literature, sculpture and architecture led humanists first to copy the tangible remains of classical times and then to appreciate them for their own sake. Dawning public awareness of the faster pace of change, coupled with loss of earlier faith in progress, has intensified attachments to tangible relics in the nineteenth and twentieth centuries.

Valued at first because of the ideals they projected, such relics then became objects of devotion and worth in their own right. They were treasured not as representative features of the past, however, but as spectacular objects precious for their cost and rarity. They were collected and protected because they were unique and peerless. And they were copied and imitated for the same reasons.

More recently, we have come to value surviving relics not merely for their symbolic references to an ideal past and because they are scarce or sumptuous, but for three other reasons: *representativeness*, for recalling the typical or characteristic traits of past epochs; *congeniality*, for providing a sense of continuity or a patina of age; and *economy*, for saving energy or materials or skills that would otherwise have to be spent on new structures. These motives sometimes conflict, sometimes overlap: landscapes may be valued both because they are unique and because they are familiar; buildings may warrant preservation both because they are symbolic and because they are elegant.

Part I of this book traces the growth of these concerns in Europe generally and in Britain in particular. We are shown how the motives that animated preservation changed with time, and the effects of those changes on the selection of structures and the means of preservation employed. But these varied from place to place as well as from epoch to epoch; comparative chronicles of preservation in various milieus are badly needed.

Both the aims and the force of preservation are specific to national and local circumstances. Britain, here treated in particular detail, is endowed with a rich sequence of relics from more than two millennia, especially from the past five centuries. No other Western country has so substantial a proportion of its landscapes, rural and urban alike, made up of recognizably historic features; no other country displays so wide a range of interest in antiquities of every kind; no other country except Greece and Italy appeals so strongly to visitors in search of the past.

Yet one of the most striking aspects of the modern impulse to preserve is its universality. The need to find, keep, and display a tangible heritage characterizes countries with an abundance of antiquities as well as those where the works of man are rare and mainly recent, countries whose regimes are communist or capitalist, former imperial powers along with newly liberated colonies. Whatever the different impulses that animate preservation in each of these places, increasing numbers of their inhabitants share a concern with their heritage. Within the past two decades this concern has engendered a host of international agencies to cater for conservation and preservation. Of these, the International Council on Monuments and Sites, under whose auspices the symposium that gave rise to this book was arranged, has pride of place. The World Heritage Convention designates sites of outstanding natural and historic interest from member countries. Architectural preservation, museum conservation, and art restoration are increasingly dealt with by technical bodies on an international basis. In many of these efforts UNESCO plays a major role.

Historic buildings have become the major focus of the preservation movement, but preservation interests embrace a multitude of other artifacts; manuscripts and motor cars, old films and steam railways each have their devotees. What role do these other relics play in our sense of our heritage? And how does our treatment of them resemble or differ from that of architectural structures? Among the myriad themes that could be explored, four are illumined in Part II of this book: prehistoric artifacts, antiques, industrial milieus, and the landscape as a whole – that largely man-made tapestry in which all our other artifacts are embedded and which give them their sense of place.

These diverse aspects of our heritage often generate comparable benefits and rewards, but the problems attending their preservation are strikingly dissimilar. Not only do the professionals concerned with industrial buildings, with landscapes, with antiques, and with archaeological sites view each of these in quite distinct ways; so does the public at large. But it is essential to recognize that our heritage is limited to no single type of object, nor to any isolated bundle of collectibles, but comprises an interdependent spectrum of relics ranging from the great collective features of the environment to the most trifling of souvenirs and personal memorabilia, and from the most enduring remains to the merest shadows of what things once were.

The task of mobilizing preservation effort differs not only between countries but also within each of them. And the burdens and rewards of preservation at the local scale often bear little resemblance to those discerned at national levels. The third part of this book presents the preservation problems of four English localities, in each of which a variety of contemporary pressures beleaguer a heritage treasured for a different reason. Comparative sketches of localities in several countries may ultimately throw light on what now often seem unexampled, and hence insoluble, difficulties. London and Paris, Khartoum and Kalamazoo, York and New York differ in their tangible heritage, but may also share needs for and abilities to sustain that heritage. Such comparisons might help us appreciate the range of risks preservation has to surmount, and the range of perspectives on which it might rely.

The growing appeal of the past we save poses its own problems – problems of maintenance, of accessibility, of interpretation, and of authenticity. This is the subject of the fourth part of our book. How to make available and intelligible to growing numbers of visitors resources that are ultimately finite is a task that perplexes governments, museum curators, private house owners, and National Trusts the world over. Public interest spurs support for preservation, and admissions help pay for upkeep and conservation, but both also magnify preservation problems. Visitors often erode the fabric of relics and sometimes threaten to destroy them altogether; popularity alters the ambience of historical appreciation and constrains ways of experiencing the past. These problems call for attention no less than the saving of antiquities from pollution and development. There is little point in 'saving' the past if what is saved is debased or altered beyond recognition.

What lies ahead for historic preservation? Conflicting predictions are constantly made. On the one hand, preservation is said to be a fad of the moment fuelled by nostalgia for more progressive or peaceful epochs; on the other, it is seen as a harbinger of a permanently resource- and heritage-conscious world. The future of the past cannot be foretold. But the essays in this book make clear that the scope of preservation has fundamentally changed. That change is irreversible. Now that preservation is concerned with the whole fabric of the country – the familiar residues of the everyday past, humble as well as great, recent along with remote – it can never again be limited to an appreciation of unique architectural masterpieces. Now that preservation is the concern of millions of ordinary folk who take pleasure and pride from the relics of their own and others' pasts, it can no longer be the exclusive province of a small elite. And now that preservation is substantially justified as a means of husbanding scarce energy and material resources, it can no longer be regarded solely as an aesthetic extra, a romantic quest to secure beauty and variety from the past against the ugly monotony of today.

All this said, the aesthetic component of preservation remains highly significant. The preservation movement opens our eyes and hearts to what lies around us, enhancing our own surroundings by encouraging concern about them. As we save what is good from the past, we realize we need not be passive passers-by, but can be active participants both in securing and in remaking the world we have inherited.

Introduction

FURTHER READING

Chamberlin, E. R. *Preserving the Past*. London: J. M. Dent & Sons, 1979. Thoughtful and lively survey of the global preoccupation with saving – and often with moving – the physical remains of the past, ranging from Abu Simbel and Masada to the Elgin Marbles and the Benin bronzes, Westminster Abbey and London Bridge in Arizona.

Cormack, Patrick. *Heritage in Danger*. London and New York: Quartet Books, 1978. General background to preservation in Britain, with chapters on the countryside, the country house, cities and villages, artists and craftsmen, patrons and public collections, followed by a county-by-county gazetteer.

Davis, Fred. *Yearning for Yesterday: A Sociology of Nostalgia*. New York and London: Collier Macmillan/Free Press, 1979. The conditions and circumstances that evoke nostalgia for the past, its functions in the face of personal and social change, and its consequences for society as a whole.

Faulkner, P.A. 'A Philosophy for the Preservation of our Historic Heritage' (three Bossom Lectures), *Journal of the Royal Society of Arts*, Vol. 126 (1978), pp. 452-80. The former chief of ancient monuments and historic buildings in Britain's Department of the Environment defines and evaluates the historic heritage, discusses the problem of preserving it without impairing its significance, and offers a preservation philosophy that takes into account aims from recording building details to physical retention.

Fawcett, Jane (ed.). *The Future of the Past: Attitudes to Conservation, 1174-1974*. London: Thames & Hudson for the Victorian Society, 1976. Essays by Pevsner, Betjeman, Girouard, Casson and others on developing attitudes to the preservation of buildings, mainly in Britain.

Historic Preservation Today: Essays Presented to the Seminar on Preservation and Restoration: Williamsburg, Virginia, 1963. Charlottesville, Va.: The University Press of Virginia for the National Trust for Historic Preservation and Colonial Williamsburg, Inc., 1966. Pioneering studies of European and American experiences in saving, rehabilitating, and displaying historic buildings.

Hosmer, Charles B., Jr. *Presence of the Past: A History of the Preservation Movement in the United States before Williamsburg*. New York: G. P. Putnam's Sons, 1965. Fascinating account of the early pioneering days of American preservation, from Mount Vernon in the 1850s to the 1920s.

Hosmer, Charles B., Jr. *Preservation Comes of Age: from Williamsburg to the National Trust, 1926-1949*. Charlottesville, Va.: University Press of Virginia for the Preservation Press, 1981. Carries the history of American preservation forward from the first conservation efforts, the rise of outdoor museums, and battles by local groups to save key landmarks, to the start of a federally-supported nationwide movement.

Kain, Roger (ed.). *Planning for Conservation*. London: Mansell, 1981. Essays on various aspects of rural and urban conservation in Canada, Germany, Austria, Poland, Greece, France, and Britain, from a 1977 International Conference on the History of Urban and Regional Planning.

Lynch, Kevin. *What Time Is This Place?* Cambridge, Mass., and London: MIT Press, 1972. How the feeling of time merges with the sense of place, and how the sense of the past in a city relates to what is conserved – or destroyed.

Morton, Terry B. (ed.). *Monumentum*, Vol. 13, Washington, D.C.: Preservation Press for US/ICOMOS, 1976. Historical, legal, technological, and touristic aspects of preservation in the United States as undertaken by federal agencies and non-governmental organizations.

National Trust for Historic Preservation. *Preservation: Toward an Ethic in the 1980s.* Washington, D.C.: Preservation Press, 1980. Goals and future directions for public agencies and the private sector emerging from a 1979 National Preservation Conference at Williamsburg.

Newcomb, Robert M. *Planning the Past: Historical Landscape Resources and Recreation*. Folkestone, Kent: Dawson; Hamden, Conn.: Archon Books/The Shoe String Press, 1979. How to inventory and manage resources from the visible past for recreational purposes, with case studies from Britain, Denmark, and the United States.

Timmons, Sharon (ed.). *Preservation and Conservation: Principles and Practices*. Washington, D.C.: Smithsonian Institution Press for the Preservation Press, 1976. Comprehensive review, categorized into series of papers dealing with occupations and organizations, materials and techniques, and philosophy, standards, and education for preservation.

Part I

CARING FOR THE PAST:
CHANGING ATTITUDES

THE PAST has always exerted powerful pressure on the present. Since time immemorial men have paid homage to the memories and deeds of their ancestors, linking themselves with their forebears through myth, tradition, and history. This attachment to times past has also embraced ancient artifacts and works of art.

Interest in the material past has been translated into a serious and systematic effort to conserve it only in recent centuries, however, as the essays in this part show. Not until the early nineteenth century did Europeans and Americans strongly identify themselves with their material heritage, and only within the past half-century have most countries come to promote preservation as a positive public programme.

Present-day preservation stems from a three-fold awareness of the past: that it was unlike the present, that it is crucial to our sense of identity, and that its tangible remnants are rapidly disappearing. So swift is the pace of change today, so glaringly apparent are the differences between the present and even the recent past, that we are apt to overlook the fact that such consciousness is a new experience. During most of human history people have lived under much the same circumstances as their immediate and even remote forebears, major change has occurred at an imperceptible pace, and past has scarcely been differentiated from present.

Not until the Renaissance did a sense of the historical past as a set of separate realms become habitual, even among the educated. A crucial element in Renaissance

17

esteem of classical antiquity – and of determination to revive its virtues – was the belief that antiquity was set off from the present by a more recent and inferior past. The Renaissance legacy over the next four centuries spread to encompass most aspects of European culture, infusing education, forms of government, art, literature, and material structures with classical features, themes, and precepts.

Given this attachment to the past, how was it that the preservation of surviving antiquities so long attracted so little interest? Renaissance and later admirers of Greece and Rome were more apt to plunder ancient structures and temples to get raw materials for their own creations than to conserve them as relics. Although they were devoted preservers of the records and literature of classical antiquity, they felt no need to hang on to its material remnants and ruins.

A concern for preserving the material past, as opposed simply to imitating and vying with it, required the further insights Michael Hunter describes. Physical relics of the past came to matter in their own right only when it became clear that the history of each epoch and nation, indeed of each individual, was unique. As long as human nature was seen as everywhere the same, history was treated as a vast mine of exemplary episodes from which to draw lessons, and material evidence of the past served no special purpose. Only with the rise of historicism, when men in different times and places were seen to be actuated in distinctively unique ways, did material relics become an essential adjunct of historical study and a prime source of empathetic understanding of the past.

Several late-eighteenth and early-nineteenth century developments reinforced the emotional and symbolic importance of relics. One was the sense of folk identity in Europe's emergent nation-states, whose vernacular languages, folklore, antiquities, and material arts provided a focus for national self-consciousness. Relics were revered, preserved, and where necessary invented as symbols of national and social aspirations. The rediscovery of sites and treasures from the cradles of European civilization in the Nile and the Mediterranean stimulated both scholarly and popular interest in material remains. A new awareness of individual identity encouraged men to view life as a career, looking back for meaning and comfort to childhood scenes and treasuring souvenirs of remembered places. Concomitantly, ruins and ancient relics served as reminders of evanescence and mortality; for romantics, whatever was old took on an aesthetic or sentimental appeal. And revulsion against widespread destructive change, signalled first by the excesses of the French Revolution, Hunter notes, led increasing numbers to view with fearful concern the transformations induced by the Industrial Revolution. Men had similarly mourned previous devastations, such as that caused in the sixteenth century by the dissolution of the English monasteries, but only in the nineteenth century did the sense of material loss become pervasive.

Preservation interests have proliferated in our own time largely because these forces have all intensified. Resurgent tribal and local loyalties require the reaffirmation of symbolic links with the material past. Psychology and psychoanalysis emphasize the significance of links with our personal past. And the pace of technological change, the radical modernization of the built environment, the speed of material obsolescence, an increasing propensity to migrate to new homes, and greater longevity combine to leave us in ever less familiar environments; we are remote even from our own recently remembered past. In a world grown so strange, we hunger for the sense of permanence that tangible relics can best provide. Prevailing doubts – disaffection with modern structures, pessimism about the future – add fuel to nostalgia for the past, which has so lengthened and deepened that we now treasure and preserve the remains of the everyday and the familiar, along with the monumental and magnificent relics, of all epochs.

How the values perceived in past forms and structures have affected their disposition and use is Hugh Prince's theme. His illustrations from sixteenth- to nineteenth-century England illumine comparable situations elsewhere. He shows that energetic Elizabethans used newly-made fortunes to build dwellings in a classical style that displayed their membership in a cultured elite. In like spirit nineteenth-century Americans used neoclassical forms and ornament-ation to civilize the wilderness. A self-confident and inventive classicism in both cases stamped a latter-day landscape with lineaments loosely borrowed from a little-known, and often vastly altered, antiquity.

The shift from Jacobean pastiche to precise Palladianism and the respectful neoclassicism of the early nineteenth century parallels the later transition from Gothick whimsy to academic medievalism. The more carefully and faithfully ancient models were imitated and replicated, the more the originals came to matter for their own sake. The sequence from loose and unself-conscious borrowing, to rigorous and scholarly imitation, to the preservation of original antiquities recurs again and again in the history of taste.

Antiquities in mid-Victorian England were not simply preserved, however; they were restored and 'improved'. Architects motivated by a religious or moral aesthetic stripped a large number of buildings, especially churches, of later accretions and restored them to the purity they were believed to have had, or that restorers felt they ought to have had.

The 'anti-scrape' reaction to these mutilations, first sounded by John Ruskin in 1848 and adopted as an article of faith by William Morris and the Society for the Protection of Ancient Buildings in 1877, has made preservation in England increasingly respectful of surviving structures as faithful repositories of human experience. Antiquities were not to be altered to conform with modern views of purity or propriety, but to be maintained unchanged as legacies from the past to the future. Different standards apply, to be sure, for ancient buildings adapted to new uses.

Prince suggests here that preservation so strictly construed may lack the improvisation and adaptability needed to come to terms with the implacable pressures of present-day development; but it is no less true that without an exemplary past, truthfully and generously preserved, the present will lack models to inspire it and the future be deprived of organic links with both past and present.

CHAPTER 1

The Preconditions of Preservation: A Historical Perspective

MICHAEL HUNTER

ALL MATTERS of current concern tend to spawn a fashionable curiosity about their origins. Preservation is no exception. Growing public interest in the subject has inspired a number of accounts of the history of our present policy and attitudes, and the best of these are listed at the end of this chapter. Nonetheless, there is room for a fresh look at the topic. In my view, many previous accounts of the subject have been rather one-sided. Disproportionate emphasis has often been placed on what is really a relatively minor episode, the question of restoration and anti-restoration, of 'scrape and anti-scrape', particularly in Victorian England. Dr J. M. Crook recently declared, when comparing the experience of the twentieth century with that of the nineteenth, that 'the enemy is no longer the restorer but the destroyer' (*Times Literary Supplement,* 22 July 1977, p. 887). But in fact the destroyer has always been the main enemy of the preservationist movement, and questions of taste and technique in restoration, though not important, are essentially subordinate. For this reason I shall be virtually ignoring them here.

Furthermore, many existing surveys seem to me rather narrow and hagiographic, placing disproportionate emphasis on a few pioneers – such as John Ruskin and William Morris – and neglecting their background. Here, by contrast, I shall stress broad trends in Britain and on the Continent, and individuals will appear only incidentally. Along with habitual neglect of all but the best-known pioneers has gone an equally misleading tendency to attach undue

22

significance to isolated early examples of preservation and to prophetic pleas for preservation which were far in advance of their time. It is possible to find occasional evidence of forms of 'conservation' in the Middle Ages, if not earlier, while regrets about the destruction of venerable structures may be chronicled equally far back. This has been especially true of remarkable buildings like the Colosseum; can one not read 'preservationist' overtones into the saying, recorded in the Dark Ages, that *quandiu stat Colisaeus, stat et Roma*, 'so long as the Colosseum stands, so will Rome'? Yet excessive emphasis on the exceptional obscures the rarity of conservationist attitudes until quite recently and disguises a decisive shift that has occurred in recent centuries. This shift, in my view, is the proper focus for a history of modern preservationist attitudes.

Two things are crucial. One is the growth of the view that the preservation of ancient monuments should be ensured deliberately rather than left to chance. The other is the extension of this view to a sizeable enough sector of influential opinion in a country for such an aspiration to be applied in practice. Monuments had been preserved before this occurred and many have been destroyed since, but a national conviction that such matters should be methodically supervised and controlled was crucial. It ensured such characteristic activities, now common but once unheard-of, as full and careful recording of old buildings and field antiquities, constant vigilance to prevent their deterioration, legislation penalizing vandalism, and taking monuments into public ownership to prevent desecration or destruction. These are the hallmarks of systematic preservation, and it is the history of this policy that should be traced rather than random examples of preservationist feeling since the beginning of time.

Systematic preservation is, on the whole, a nineteenth-century and twentieth-century phenomenon. Its beginnings were outlined by the art historian Gerald Baldwin Brown, whose *Care of Ancient Monuments* (1905) gives details of the legislation passed and public or private institutions established to preserve and record ancient sites and buildings in Europe and elsewhere. There were a few precursors. Italy has had more or less effectual preservationist measures since the Renaissance; Sweden adopted pioneering codes in the seventeenth century, some other countries in the eighteenth. But the early nineteenth century was the decisive time for the inauguration of such policies in Europe. In Denmark a Royal Commission for antiquities was established in 1807, and what John Harvey described in *Conservation of Buildings* (1972, p. 27) as 'the first general decree dealing with the whole problem of architectural monuments' was issued by Ludwig I, Grand Duke of Hesse, in 1818. Similar measures followed in Prussia and other German states in the following decades; in France in the 1830s an Inspectorate and a Commission were set up which did much for the cause of preservation; in Italy newly systematic measures were implemented in the early nineteenth century. One of the first acts of the newly independent kingdom of Greece was a monument law of 1834 based on the conviction that 'all objects of antiquity in Greece, as the productions of the ancestors of the Hellenic people, are regarded as the common national possession of all Hellenes' (Brown, p. 217). These early measures were subsequently consolidated, preservationist legislation reaching a climax around 1900.

Similar developments came in Britain only towards the end of the nineteenth century, despite increasingly vociferous protest from the eighteenth century onwards. Sir John Lubbock's bill for the preservation of ancient monuments first appeared in Parliament in 1873 and William Morris's celebrated Society for the Protection of Ancient Buildings was founded in 1877. Preservationist machinery began with the Ancient Monuments Act of 1882 and subsequent legislation; with the foundation of the National Trust in 1895; and with growing civic concern, London setting a precedent not only in recording buildings through the London Survey but also in preserving them.

Why was it in the nineteenth century that this took

place? All this legislation and organization should be seen in the context of the growing power of central and local government that was so characteristic of nineteenth-century Europe. But though this explains why it was possible for such a programme to be implemented at the time, it does not explain why people felt that the preservation of old buildings and sites was a suitable subject for state intervention. There had been powerful and centralized states before which had never bothered with such legislation; nor was all such activity in the nineteenth century associated with the state. The legislation reflected and resulted from a consensus of informed opinion which had not previously existed, and whose causes must be sought elsewhere.

An important factor in the growth of consensus was the popularization and vulgarization of an interest in the past, part of a broader spread of education and leisure in the eighteenth and nineteenth centuries. One can trace a rise of tourism, of a more or less well-informed curiosity about sites and buildings, beginning in the Renaissance period, spreading among the fashionable in the seventeenth and eighteenth centuries, and becoming genuinely popular in the nineteenth. Antiquarianism likewise became first genteel and then popular in the nineteenth century, as reflected in the growing market for books on historical topics, the spread of museums, and the proliferation of historical societies. By the nineteenth century more people were susceptible to the intrinsic interest of the relics of the past than ever before, and this is a trend accelerated by the mass media in the twentieth century.

But this growing popular interest in antiquities leaves something unexplained, for what really mattered was not just the number of people interested in history, but the nature of their attitude towards the past and the value that they put on its relics. A particular sense of the past underlay the onset of systematic preservation, and this may be illuminated by surveying general views of the past and their implications for preservation.

Preservation depends on some kind of feeling that

earlier epochs of our own or other cultures have something to offer the present. This feeling may be confused and uncritical: many of the attitudes underlying popular support for preservation today have much in common with the vague respect for antiquity that has existed since time immemorial, inspiring much random preservation over the centuries. If the history of preservation comprised no more than the changing fortunes of this awed or nostalgic adulation of antiquity, it would hardly be worth writing about except as a symptom of a more general and perennial appeal to the past that has been well surveyed by J. H. Plumb in *The Death of the Past* (1969).

But in recent centuries, such attitudes have been significantly modified. In the first place, since the Renaissance an approach to the past has gained ground, essentially antagonistic to such uncritical views of older times yet also with preservationist overtones. This is the sense of 'history' of which modern scholarship is the heir, characterized by a preoccupation with historical change, an acute sense of anachronism and a stress on the importance of the accurate study of past periods, often undermining their sentimental appeal (hence the 'death' chronicled by Plumb). Those who adopted this perspective have typically placed a high premium on original and authentic historical sources as the only means of reconstructing earlier epochs, thus giving an impetus to the conservation of such evidence, whether written or tangible. Protests against destruction – usually ineffectual – will be found in the writings of antiquaries from the Renaissance onwards. The earliest extant English plea for systematic preservation was made by Richard Gough, Director of the Society of Antiquaries, in the *Gentleman's Magazine* in 1788, on the ground that old buildings should be kept as materials for historical study. Historical research was a stimulus for preservation of a systematic kind that had hitherto been lacking. But it was a minority view, and its effect on policy and practice was limited.

Erudition was not the only trend antagonistic to traditional, respectful views of the past that post-Renaissance Europe fostered. For while historical study gradually undermined traditional awe of antiquity, a much more direct assault against the past came from another intellectual movement: the rationalism and progressivism associated with the rise of modern science in the sixteenth and seventeenth centuries and the Enlightenment of the eighteenth. The appeal to reason and confidence in the perfectibility of all things through the removal of superstition and obfuscation were directly antagonistic to a concern with the past. Whereas destruction had always been common, it had previously lacked the articulate rationale with which it was now provided. The result is to be seen in the increasing inroads made on relics of the past by what John Carter, an English antiquary of the eighteenth century, bewailed in the *Gentleman's Magazine* (1798, p. 1104) as 'the innovating system for improving (as it is called) our cities and towns'.

Such destruction reached its climax in the French Revolution and the subsequent revolutionary wars that engulfed Europe. The reaction that these brought strengthened a rival tradition of thought that had been growing in the eighteenth century, particularly in Germany. This was the view often referred to as 'historicism', hailed by the historian Friedrich Meinecke's *Enstehung des Historismus* (1936) as one of the 'greatest revolutions in human thought'. Historicism challenged the Enlightenment's confidence in abstract reason and universal progress and, arguing that history offered the only proper key to understanding all human phenomena, provided a new justification for the historical erudition that had flourished since the Renaissance.

Historicist views enjoyed immense influence in all areas of European thought in the nineteenth century, and had important implications for preservation. For the stress placed by historicist thinkers on the uniqueness of historical change – which, in the nineteenth century, took on strong nationalist overtones – gave great significance to the origins and development of nations and localities as keys to their distinctive character. When the national past was seen as enriching the present through tradition and continuity, tangible relics of previous epochs acquired urgent importance as visible guarantors of historical identity, which it was essential to safeguard against the arbitrary standardization which the revolutionary wars seemed to threaten. These attitudes to some extent overlapped with perennial nostalgia about the past, and precursors may be found, especially in smaller countries with earlier incentives to safeguard the historic guarantees of their identity. But views of this kind now became commoner and more potent, and their influence was further increased by the current mood of romanticism, involving the imaginative reconstruction of past times in all their unique and picturesque detail and mystery.

The historicist inspiration of preservationist activity in the early nineteenth century was quite explicit. The 1818 pioneering measure of Ludwig I of Hesse opened with the statement: 'Whereas the surviving monuments of architecture are among the most important and interesting evidence of history, in that from them may be inferred the former customs, culture, and civil condition of the nation, and therefore their preservation is greatly to be wished, we decree as follows...' Historicist sentiments found frequent echoes in preservationist contexts. For example, at a congress held at Strasbourg in 1899, attention to preservation was urged as 'a question of life and death for the historical sciences and for the maintenance of the national consciousness' (G. B. Brown, p. 99).

In Britain the influence of historicism came rather late, reaching a peak only in the 1870s. Its context was the erosion of simple-minded progressivism, partly by the intellectual crisis of the post-Darwinian years, partly by the Great Depression and Britain's increasingly disappointing industrial performance. By 1890 Havelock Ellis in *The New Spirit* (p. 24) envisioned England not as a centre of industry and commerce but as 'a museum of antiquities'. It is not surprising to find preservationist measures and organizations first appearing in Britain in the 1870s just when historicist sentiment was making itself felt in other ways in official circles – for instance in a growing valuation of the customary seen in Gladstone's Irish and Scottish Land Acts. Nor is it surprising that the sentiments underlying preservation echo contemporary German historicist views. These sentiments are epitomized in Morris's view, expressed in the 1877 letter to the *Athenaeum* that sparked off the SPAB, that ancient churches were 'sacred monuments of the nation's growth and hope'.

But though the 1870s saw the beginning of change in England, it gathered strength slowly, attesting to the endurance of *laissez-faire* sentiment so characteristic of Victorian England. Sir John Lubbock's Ancient Monuments bill reappeared so many times in Parliament that it became known as the 'monumentally ancient bill': the objections to it boiled down to Warton's predictable complaint in 1882 that it would involve 'invasion of rights of property... in order to gratify the antiquarian tastes of a few at the public expense'. The strength of such attitudes in 1905 is shown by the defensive tone in which Brown's *The Care of Ancient Monuments* described official intervention to prevent the demolition of a fine building in Bavaria; he was afraid that many in Britain would find this 'a lordly way of doing things' (pp. 117-18), though it would now appear commonplace.

But attitudes were already changing and state and municipal intervention becoming increasingly common in social welfare and related fields as the inadequacy of earlier *laissez-faire* policies became apparent. This partly provides the context for the acceleration of preservationist organization and activity in Britain, but equally important was a growing sense of urgent need due to widespread demolition. In this there may be some parallel with the destruction experienced on the Continent during and after the wars early in the century, reflected in the articulate complaints of Victor Hugo and others.

In England a growing sense of scarcity evidently underlay both Lubbock's preservation bill and Morris's preservation society. Most striking, however, is the case of London, where destruction for rebuilding reached alarming levels at the end of the nineteenth century and preservationist activity reached a climax as a result. It was associated especially with the London Survey Committee, which, in C. R. Ashbee's introduction to its volume on Bromley-by-Bow in 1900, drew up a horrifying list of buildings in and about the city that had been demolished or threatened in the previous decade on account of 'the immediate requirements of the moment'. The threatened destruction of the Trinity Hospital at Mile End (the subject of the Survey's first publication, also edited by Ashbee, in 1896) caused particular alarm; it illustrated not only the need for preservation but also the related need for record, since few had previously known of the building's existence despite the importance of its associations and architectural interest to 'national history'. Gladstone commented in the Trinity Hospital volume on 'the barbarous work... and the desecration' that the city was suffering (p. 28), and public opinion was clearly ready to support a more constructive attitude to preservation. In 1897 the London County Council gave its official (and financial) support to the London Survey, whose objective, as its 1900 volume made clear, was 'not so much the making of a *paper* record, as the preservation of the things recorded'. In 1900 the LCC set another precedent by taking into public ownership a historic building threatened with destruction, the Inner Temple gateway in Fleet Street.

This metropolitan initiative set the pattern for wider developments. When the Ancient Monuments Act of 1882 was renewed in 1900 its effectiveness was extended, and the new Act passed in 1913 went further still, giving the state genuine pre-emptive powers. Meanwhile the London Survey was matched in 1908 by its national equivalent, the Royal Commission on Historical Monuments. Such measures provided the matrix within which systematic preservation has been organized in Britain ever since.

What is more, this pioneering episode displays in microcosm many of the components of the present British situation: a feeling of pressing urgency against a background of historicist sentiment informed by a wider unease at the direction in which things were moving.

If this perspective on our current position is illuminating, the conclusions that one may draw from it are not optimistic, however. Most disquieting is the sheer reluctance with which relevant measures were implemented in this country – a reluctance not without its contemporary equivalent. More generally, the elaboration of sporadic precedents into a systematic preservationist policy has depended on a historicist reaction against simplistic progressivism which is both recent and precarious. There remains no shortage of heirs to the Enlightenment prophets who proclaimed the past and its relics irrelevant. Even today historicist values inspire only a minority, though disillusionment with the values of modern society yearly swells its ranks. Our task, therefore, is a large one: we have not only to assert the relevance of the past but, at the same time, to ensure that its tangible relics survive as the materials of historical study and as guarantors of historical identity for our descendants.

FURTHER READING

Briggs, M. S. *Goths and Vandals: a Study of the Destruction, Neglect and Preservation of Historical Buildings in England.* London: Constable, 1952. Entertaining narrative.

Brown, Gerard Baldwin. *The Care of Ancient Monuments.* Cambridge: University Press, 1905. Still very valuable survey of nineteenth-century preservationist legislation and institutional activity.

Burke, Peter. *The Renaissance Sense of the Past.* London: Edward Arnold, 1969. Brief introduction to Renaissance changes, incorporating documentary sources.

Bury, J. B. *The Idea of Progress: An Inquiry into its Origin and Growth.* London: Macmillan, 1920; reprinted, New York: Dover, 1955. Classic study of the development of a view of history as linear and irreversible.

Fawcett, Jane (ed.). *The Future of the Past: Attitudes to Conservation, 1174-1974.* London: Thames & Hudson for the Victorian Society, 1976. Interesting studies by various eminent authors.

Caring for the Past: Changing Attitudes

Harvey, John H. *Conservation of Buildings*. London: John Baker, 1972. Provides useful data on preservation attitudes.

Hunter, Michael. 'Germanic and Roman Antiquity and the Sense of the Past in Anglo-Saxon England', *Anglo-Saxon England*, Vol. 3 (1974), pp. 29-50. Case-study of traditional attitudes to relics of the past.

Kennet, Wayland. *Preservation*. London: Maurice Temple Smith, 1972. Chatty and informative historical summary of preservation, followed by accounts of case histories in England.

Madsen, Stephan T. *Restoration and Anti-Restoration: A Study in English Restoration Philosophy*. Oslo: Universitetsforlaget, 1976; 1981 reprint under the name of Stephan Tschudi-Madsen. Detailed study of nineteenth-century attitudes, notably in Britain.

Plumb, J. H. *The Death of the Past*. London: Macmillan, 1969; Harmondsworth: Penguin, 1973. A general background on changing attitudes to the past.

Reill, Peter Hanns. *The German Enlightenment and the Rise of Historicism*. Berkeley, Los Angeles and London: University of California Press, 1975. Valuable study of roots of nineteenth-century reaction to progressivism, in which history came to be seen as of transcendent importance in understanding human experience.

CHAPTER 2

Revival, Restoration, Preservation: Changing Views about Antique Landscape Features

HUGH PRINCE

THE CONFLICT between a wish to build anew for present and future uses and a desire to save what is old because it adds to the heritage of a place may be resolved by reviving, restoring or preserving genuinely old or old-style landscape features. New buildings may be designed to look old by reproducing period styles of architecture or decoration. That is revival. Old buildings may be made to serve new uses or their appearance may be improved by replacing obsolete or ugly parts. That is restoration. Old buildings may be protected and simply maintained in good repair. That is preservation. The past may also be evoked or commemorated by place-names or historical associations after the original landscape features have disappeared. In different periods people have expressed their attachment to the past by making and keeping relics and ancient monuments. This essay attempts to account for differing attitudes towards the past taken by English Renaissance, romantic and Victorian designers and observers.

Landscapes of the Renaissance, 1540–1680

During the sixteenth and seventeenth centuries, a bourgeois ruling class displaced a feudal aristocracy. The new rulers cut their ties with the authorities from whom their predecessors had derived political strength. They seized power from families holding Norman pedigrees and they demilitarized baronial castles. They severed links with the Church of

Rome and pulled down hundreds of monasteries. Amassing immense wealth from acquisitions of monastic land, securing privileges through practice in law, vested with extensive executive powers by Tudor monarchs, the new dynasts founded estates that were expected to yield increasing incomes to their children and grandchildren and they designed houses to last many generations. They used new-gained wealth to clear woods, to drain marshes, to reclaim heaths, to sink coal pits, to reorganize iron and woollen cloth manufacturing and to engage in overseas trade. Having broken away from feudal society and renounced medieval Catholicism, the new lords found a source of knowledge and inspiration in Renaissance scholarship.

Courtiers, lawyers, country gentlemen and Anglican clergymen displayed their classical learning to affirm that they belonged to a civilized elite. They wrote scholarly treatises, used Latin syntax in learned writing, applied the canons of Greek philosophy to science and politics, observed Euclidean principles in geometry and studied the five classical orders in architecture. A classical education gave them the keys to power in the present and, through mathematics and astronomy, promised a means of anticipating the future. Familiarity with classical literature and mythology spread beyond the ruling class, providing material for popular entertainment and private recreations. Playwrights assumed that their audiences would recognize allusions to characters drawn from Greek and Roman legends and would know about incidents in ancient history. A taste for classical decoration diffused rapidly and widely among those who were rebuilding or enlarging their houses. Local styles of building gave way to the fashionable accents of Renaissance Italy and the Low Countries. Perishable thatch and wattle and daub were banished from the homes of the rich. Walls were built of durable brick and faced with stone, roofs were tiled, gutters were wrought of lead or iron and interiors were lit by large glazed windows. Stonework was elaborately carved with classical motifs.

Many people, educated in newly-founded grammar

schools and colleges at Oxford and Cambridge, began to collect, study and copy antique objects. As early as the 1540s, Henry VIII's Treasurer, Sir John Cuttes, built Salisbury Hall, a moated manor house near Shenley in Hertfordshire. The exterior is more traditional than modern, but the hallway is adorned with large medallions of Roman emperors, faithfully imitating Roman low-reliefs. By the 1560s, Elizabethan courtiers were outbidding each other in the richness of ornamentation applied to the outside of their houses. Queen Elizabeth's Secretary, Sir William Cecil, built a palace at Theobalds near Cheshunt, heavily ornamented with classical columns, arches and pediments. Cecil's brother-in-law and lifelong political rival, Sir Nicholas Bacon, built a mansion at Gorhambury near St Albans. A highly ornate classical porch carried Ionic and Tuscan columns, inlaid marble panels and Roman figures in the niches. At the beginning of the seventeenth century, Charlton House, Holland House, Hatfield, Cassiobury, Audley End, Blickling and other splendid houses built by successful lawyers, wealthy merchants and rising gentry were sumptuously furnished with classical ornaments. Although heavily encrusted with classical features, Jacobean mansions looked distinctively English and unashamedly new. Their style was modern; their classicism was added as surface decoration.

Gardens as well as houses were designed on regular, symmetrical lines and adorned with classical ornaments. At Theobalds, gardens laid out in the 1580s contained a fountain at the centre, canals, a banqueting house, busts of Roman emperors and a labyrinth of Venus. In the 1630s, at Little Hadham, a Hertfordshire squire, Sir Arthur Capel, created an Italianate garden embellished with fountains and statuary. Later in the century, Sir William Temple praised the epicurean garden at Moor Park as 'the perfectest Figure of a Garden I ever saw'; he particularly admired the disposition of two terraces cut into the slope of a hill and the arrangement of walks, parterres and a grotto. These designs can scarcely be compared with the magnificent

Italian Renaissance gardens of the Vatican Belvedere, of the Villa d'Este or of Pratolino, but they introduced a note of classical order and formality into the English landscape. Renaissance patrons borrowed freely from history but only from a narrowly selected period. Medieval art was despised and neglected. Some welcomed the destruction of monasteries and the dispersal of medieval libraries not only as means of purging the country of graven images and popish superstition but also as a liberation from artistic ignorance. Towards the end of the sixteenth century attitudes began to soften. Some Elizabethan scholars cautiously acknowledged the value of studying medieval history and appreciated the importance of materials that had survived. But long after historians rediscovered the range and depth of medieval thought, prejudice against medieval decorative art persisted. In 1697, in his *Account of Architects and Architecture*, the diarist John Evelyn scorned Gothic 'congestions of heavy, dark, melancholy and *Monkish Piles*', with 'slender and misquine *Pillars*... ponderous arched Roofs... sharp *Angles, Jetties,* narrow *Lights,* lame *Statues, Lace* and other *Cut-Work* and *Crickle-Crankle*'. Gothic forms were already returning to favour when Evelyn wrote, but echoes of that derogatory attitude were heard as late as 1771, when Smollett's old-fashioned Mr Bramble in *Humphrey Clinker* complained: 'The external appearance of an old cathedral cannot but be displeasing to the eye of every man who has any idea of propriety and proportion'.

The prestige, power and fortunes of Renaissance aristocrats lasted no longer than those of their feudal predecessors. Dynasties set up to rule for ever toppled as fast as one monarch succeeded another or one set of favourites was ousted by others. Even bishops and judges were unseated when doctrine and constitution were amended. When the king himself was beheaded in 1649, all pretence of permanence finally vanished. During the Civil War houses belonging to both sides were pillaged and demolished. While royalists sacked Ashridge and drove deer out of the park, parliamentarians allowed their soldiery to pull down

Theobalds and carry away the stones. Thomas Fuller commented that 'from the seat of a monarch it is now become a little commonwealth; so may entire tenements, like splinters, have flown out of the materials thereof. Thus our fathers saw it built, we behold it unbuilt'. Many families ennobled by the Tudors and enriched by mercantile fortunes were displaced two or three generations later by others rising from the same origins. At the end of the seventeenth century, only 42 out of 395 Hertfordshire manors remained in possession of the families who owned them in 1540. As new families of patrons succeeded one another, their devotion to classicism became more serious and more refined.

Early in the seventeenth century, a pure, disciplined style based on a close study of Roman and Italian Renaissance buildings was introduced into England by Inigo Jones. He graduated from sketching stage sets for royal masques to building the first correctly proportioned Renaissance villa in England. In 1616, he designed Queen's House at Greenwich and in 1619 he started work on a Banqueting Hall in Whitehall which was to form part of a full-sized Renaissance palace. The Whitehall scheme remained un-finished and Inigo Jones turned his hand to planning a layout for an arcaded piazza and a Doric temple on the Earl of Bedford's estate at Covent Garden. Outside London, few houses were designed in a strict Palladian style until early in the eighteenth century.

English Renaissance architecture broke with medieval and vernacular traditions, but did not fully embrace classical traditions. Little respect was shown for surviving ancient monuments. In addition to the wholesale demolition of monastic buildings and other medieval structures, sections of London's Roman wall were plundered for stone, and Roman masonry in the walls of Colchester Castle was bombarded by parliamentarian cannons. Sixteenth- and early-seventeenth-century antiquaries robbed graves, collected coins, metalwork, pottery and curios, and cata-logued their finds. They were more interested in treasure-hunting than in seeking to understand past cultures. English Renaissance patrons were not deeply attached to the past.

In a vain search for immortality, or at least to make their mark on recorded history, the new elite paid heralds, genealogists and local historians to connect their families with aristocratic lineages and to trace the descent of their manors. And in a country where few structures lasted longer than a generation, mapmakers and topographers explored and delineated in detail the sites and forms of ancient remains. Following the appearance in 1540 of John Leland's *Itinerary*, a systematic search for antiquities began. Leland was guided on his travels by accounts of classical authors and medieval chroniclers. He paid no attention to Stonehenge or other monuments of prehistory. William Camden's *Britannia*, 1586, not only examined prehistoric relics but amplified the evidence of literary descriptions with the evidence of coins, inscriptions and place-names. Camden's work, translated into English and edited by later scholars, held a leading place among topographical surveys for over two centuries. Neither Leland nor Camden attempted to reconstruct the geographical, economic and social conditions of the past. In *Ruins in a Landscape* (p. 15), Stuart Piggott reminds us that 'we have to wait until after the Civil War before we really see the beginning of antiquarianism of the kind which was then to persist well into the nineteenth century'. In the second half of the seventeenth century, John Aubrey, Robert Plot, Elias Ashmole and William Dugdale made remarkable archaeological discoveries in England while Edward Lhwyd and Robert Sibbald charted Celtic origins in Wales and Scotland. Seventeenth-century antiquaries opened the eyes of educated people to the history of the stones, tracks, burial places, and fields around them. It was a great awakening.

Romantic antiquity, 1680–1830

High hopes that the restoration of Charles II would inaugurate an era of peace and prosperity were dashed by a succession of disasters early in the reign, and nearly twenty years were to pass before people began to feel secure about their future. Wounds inflicted by civil war healed slowly, fears of recurrent plagues receded gradually, plot by plot two-thirds of the city of London was rebuilt after the Great Fire and in provincial towns and seaports trade and commerce revived. In all parts of England, particularly in the south-east, capital was poured into agricultural improvements and landowners flourished. The first signs of returning confidence were expressed by the royal family and courtiers in commissioning architectural designs of majestic grandeur. The palaces, churches, college chapels and libraries designed by Christopher Wren, William Talman, William Winde, Nicholas Hawksmoor, John Vanbrugh and Thomas Archer paraded baroque splendours within precisely measured classical frameworks.

As the middle ranks of society led by landowners and merchants accumulated wealth and obtained political power baroque architecture was superseded by a less ostentatious style. Whig magnates built neat, well-proportioned villas rather than palaces. Plainness and simplicity were seen as virtues. A paragon among seventeenth-century country gentlemen, Ralph Freeman of Aspenden in Hertfordshire, son of a London merchant, was eulogized by Sir Henry Chauncy (*The Historical Antiquities of Hertfordshire* (1700), Vol. I, pp. 248-9) for having 'made his House neat, his Gardens pleasant, his Groves delicious, his Children chearful, his Servants easie, and kept excellent Order in his Family: He had general insight in Architecture and Husbandry'. He and others like him built plain, box-like houses. Travellers rejoiced at the regularity and, above all, the luxuriance of the new landscapes. They sang the praises of Ceres, Pomona and Flora for bestowing abundant crops upon well-cultivated fields. On a clear day around 1725, Daniel Defoe accompanied by two foreign visitors looked down from the heights of Bushey into the vale of St Albans. There they observed that 'the inclos'd corn fields made one grand parterre, the thick planted Hedgerows, like a Wilderness or Labyrinth divided in Espaliers; the villages interspersed looked like so many noble seats of gentlemen at a distance. In a word, it was all nature and yet look'd all art' (*A Tour Through the Whole Island of Great Britain,* Everyman edition, 1928, pp. 8-9). A multitude of settlements and small fields, tended with garden-like neatness, filled the whole length of the vale. Squareness, neatness and classical order appeared as the inseparable partners of productivity and prosperity.

As more and more of the country was laid out in a chequerboard of fields and identical farmhouses, some observers felt oppressed by the dull, monotonous repetition of regular cultivation and plodding industry. They began to question whether utility was compatible with beauty. A new generation of topographers scanned the countryside for visible reminders of primitive disorder, tracts of untamed waste or eyecatching relics. Among the first antiquaries to take a romantic view of ruins was Anthony Wood, who in 1657 at Eynsham was 'wonderfully strucken with a veneration of the stately, yet much lamented, ruins of the abbey'. At that spot he 'spent some time with a melancholy delight in taking a prospect'. The incident is recalled in an autobiographical note in *The Lives of Those Eminent Antiquaries John Leland, Thomas Hearne and Anthony à Wood* (Oxford, 1772, Vol. II, pp. 253-4). In 1708 the young William Stukeley 'frequently took a walk to sigh over the ruins of Barnwell Abbey... lamenting the destruction of so noble monuments of the Piety and Magnificence of our Ancestors'. (This is quoted by Stuart Piggott in *William Stukeley: an Eighteenth Century Antiquary*, Oxford, 1950, p. 25.) In the eighteenth century observers delighted in the decadent allure of crumbling, mossy stonework. They wallowed in the sadness of ruins set in woodland glades or reflected in silent pools, and they thrilled at the sight of broken arches or dark towers outlined against evening skies. Romantic scenes held them in suspense and played on their feelings. The Buck brothers, James Thomson, John Dyer, the young Thomas Gray, Elizabeth Montagu, Mrs Delany and a host of others turned topography into poetry, while painters made antiquity picturesque.

The objects of pictorial composition and poetic effusion were now jealously guarded as precious relics. In the early eighteenth century Stukeley complained that diggers hauled away from the sight of Verulamium 'hundreds of cartloads of Roman bricks' for road making, but a few years later the unearthing of a tesselated Roman pavement was hailed as a major discovery. Excavators went on to uncover parts of the outer ditch, wall, towers and gateways of the Roman city. In different parts of England, remains of hundreds of Roman villas were found and ancient coins and pottery were collected and carefully preserved. Relics discovered by eighteenth-century antiquaries were rarely thrown away, but many were heavily restored or turned into picturesque objects. The shell of the Norman castle at Hertford was gothicized in 1800 and at Benington Lordship a neo-Norman fantasy was fabricated to match the keep of Benington castle. No attempt was made to separate genuine from imitation antiques.

A search for ruins kept dozens of learned antiquarians fully occupied, but the fashionable demand for picturesque towers and follies far exceeded the supply of genuine antiquities and stretched the powers of invention of unscrupulous scholars. Builders and landscape gardeners made good the deficiencies by designing sham castles and abbeys and stone circles. Among features considered by Horace Walpole to 'indicate strongly the dawn of modern taste' was a Gothick arch at Gobions in Hertfordshire. By the end of the eighteenth century the country was generously endowed with a variety of Gothick gatehouses, Chinese pagodas, Swiss chalets, rockwork grottoes, ivy-mantled towers and cast-off ruins removed to parkland resting places. Ancient ruins possessed to a high degree the qualities prized by romantic observers: gloom and decay, mystery and melancholy, intricacy and asymmetry. Designers of sham ruins and picturesque gardens were able to reproduce these qualities and complement the pure and austere forms of Palladian architecture.

During the eighteenth century classical and Gothic styles diverged. While classical designs became more refined and more disciplined, Gothic became bolder and less restrained. At the beginning the two styles co-existed harmoniously but towards the end of the century they clashed. In the 1720s William Kent designed informal gardens with classical temples and serpentine walks as settings for strictly proportioned Palladian mansions. In the 1760s houses designed by Robert Adam required separation and distancing from parks by Lancelot Brown. The delicate modelling of the houses looked magnificent at close quarters with distant views of parkland, and the parks looked most impressive with a house glimpsed in the background. By the end of the century houses were designed in a variety of styles other than Palladian. At Ashridge James Wyatt indulged in the most exuberant mock-Perpendicular, furnishing the chapel with a fan-vaulted ceiling, in a style matching Humphry Repton's Monks' Garden. Repton's Cassiobury Park not only featured a mock-Tudor gatehouse but also a Swiss cottage to accommodate a lock-keeper on the Grand Union Canal. By 1830, towns exhibited as much architectural diversity as the country. St Albans, for example, possessed handsome red-brick Georgian town houses, a solid, plainly stuccoed Grecian town hall, Gothick almshouses, a colonial-style chapel and mock-Tudor half-timbering next door to Regency shop-fronts. Contrasting styles of architecture were held together by a general conformity of floor levels and by strong vertical accents, but no attempt was made to impose a uniform façade on different properties.

Eighteenth-century householders and shopkeepers were free and easy in their treatment of old buildings. They altered, pulled down, reconstructed and converted old structures to new uses, and they changed the exterior faces of buildings as architectural fashions changed. Well-to-do tradesmen proudly stuck Georgian brick fronts on sixteenth-century timber-framed houses, and scholarly clergymen did not hesitate to remove medieval screens, choir stalls, baroque tombs and other impedimenta in order to create a sense of lofty spaciousness and light, uniting nave and transept. If a belfry were unsound the tower might be rebuilt in Wyatt's free-style Gothick, and if a rustic porch collapsed, a stone structure might be put up in its place. Some artfully contrived additions served to heighten the historic atmosphere of a place. An eighteenth-century observer judged a restoration to be in correct taste if it evoked the spirit of the past, no matter how poorly it reproduced the original design or materials. A flight of imagination was nobler than slavish imitation.

The romantic viewpoint presented an antithesis to the calculated materialism expressed in classical architecture. In the course of the eighteenth century the fantasies of Strawberry Hill Gothick were succeeded by more faithful and more deeply respectful interpretations of the past. But the romantic vision remained free, individualistic and undogmatic. It was in the best sense permissive.

The past for its own sake, from 1830

After the Napoleonic Wars, Whig supremacy ended in a period of deep social discontent, but landed aristocrats were not sent to the guillotine nor were the institutions of government overthrown by force. Whig landowners struggled to extricate themselves from debt by marrying bankers', brewers' and nabobs' daughters, by mining coal and iron on their estates, by acquiring shares in turnpikes, canals, railways and government stock. They opened their ranks by nominating merchants and manufacturers as justices of the peace, by enlisting the sons of tradesmen as yeomanry officers and eventually by yielding to pressure for parliamentary reform. Power and influence passed into the hands of an urban and industrial bourgeoisie, and the Whig taste for Palladian or neo-classical architecture and landscape gardening was replaced by a Victorian preference for decorated Gothic or Tudor architecture and luxuriantly planted collectors' gardens. Romance was superseded by realism and utilitarianism. The new leaders of fashion museumized the past for instruction and emulation – both indoors and outdoors. They built museums and art galleries to exhibit treasures which could not be left standing outside, and they restored churches, castles and ancient monuments to enhance the historic appearance of landscapes. Genuine relics were much more highly valued than imitations, and during the Victorian period insistence upon authenticity and prohibitions against altering old structures gained in strength and intensity. The study of history was confined to an examination and verification of material remains from the past. Periods from which few objects or documents had survived were regarded as dark ages. Eighteenth-century inventiveness was condemned as fraudulent.

Dissatisfaction with imaginative reproduction of historic relics and other artifices was first intimated in polite philosophical discussions between landscape gardeners, in William Mason's *An Heroic Epistle to Sir William Chambers*, 1773, and in correspondence between Richard Payne Knight, Uvedale Price and Humphry Repton. In 1795, John Carter, quoted by Joan Evans in *A History of the Society of Antiquaries* (1956, p. 207), called for an immediate stop to James Wyatt's fanciful restorations of Gothic churches, so that Wyatt might be prevented 'from effacing the still remaining unaltered Trails of our ancient Magnificence which are but faintly to be imitated and perhaps never to be equalled'. Carter protested, in the name of truth, that no substitutes for genuine antiques could be invented. He was the first writer to raise a serious objection to the fabrication of antiquities.

The fiercest claimants for exclusive possession of truth

and authenticity in artistic taste as well as in articles of faith were rival sects of Victorian Christianity. Against the puritanical notion that nothing but the original structures would bear the stamp of truth, the high-church Camdenians sought truth and purity in a different direction. In 1845, a Camdenian writing in the *Ecclesiologist* (Vol. 4, p. 104), had 'no hesitation in urging the propriety of entirely removing late clerestories and restoring roofs to the form they undoubtedly had when the earlier arcades of the nave were built'. These nineteenth-century purists still claimed the power to convert, restore or ultimately destroy features they did not approve of. They justified their actions by asserting that the Middle Pointed represented the moral apex of medieval achievement, that earlier forms were crude and imperfect and that later forms were debased and decadent. In the second half of the nineteenth century, the restorer's licence to alter was finally revoked.

In 1849, John Ruskin in *Seven Lamps of Architecture* denounced the practice of restoration as 'a Lie from beginning to end'. He declared that 'it is... no question of expediency or feeling whether we shall preserve the buildings of past times or not. *We have no right whatever to touch them.* They are not ours. They belong partly to those who built them, and partly to all the generations of mankind who are to follow us.' Ruskin's call for an end to restoration was endorsed by the Society of Antiquaries. In 1855 the executive committee of the Society recommended that 'no restoration should ever be attempted otherwise than... in the sense of preservation from further injuries... Anything beyond this is untrue to Art, unjustifiable in taste, destructive in practice and wholly opposed to the judgement of the best Archaeologists' (Evans, *A History of the Society of Antiquaries,* p. 309). For nearly a quarter of a century after Ruskin's proclamation, churchmen and laity continued to restore churches in Gothic Revival style with unabated enthusiasm. On 5 March 1877, a letter to the *Athenaeum* from William Morris raised the issue in a sharper manner. Having learned that Tewkesbury Abbey was about to be 'destroyed' by Sir George Gilbert Scott, Morris called for an association 'to keep watch on old monuments, to protect against all "restoration" that means more than keeping out wind and weather, and by all means, literary or other, to awaken a feeling that our ancient buildings are not mere ecclesiastical toys, but sacred monuments of the nation's growth and hope'. The response was immediate. Within a few days the newly formed Society for the Protection of Ancient Buildings enlisted the support of many painters, historians and a few architects. Later in the year, J.J. Stevenson carried the attack into the lecture hall of the Royal Institution of British Architects. He declared: 'It is a delusion of restorers that their new work, because it is correctly medieval in style, is of any historical value.' Whilst Morris was primarily interested in saving medieval buildings, he objected to the destruction of seven of Wren's city churches on the ground that they formed 'a distinct link in the history of ecclesiastical art of this country' (Royal Institute of British Architects, *Sessional Papers 1876–77,* p. 219). All medieval buildings were sacrosanct, and in the course of time, official recognition and protection were accorded to Tudor, Stuart, Georgian and Regency buildings.

Since 1882, successive Ancient Monuments Protection Acts and Historic Buildings Acts have extended the powers of central and local government to survey, purchase and protect ancient monuments. The law now enshrines William Morris's principle that the public has an overriding interest in the preservation of historic buildings. Their present occupiers are regarded as 'only trustees for those who come after us'. Listed buildings may be mended and repainted but permission to alter or convert them is difficult to obtain.

In practice, it is increasingly difficult to maintain historic buildings. The ravages of weathering and woodworm bite deeper into the fabric of walls and roofs as they grow older and calls for more extensive and more radical repairs recur more frequently. At the same time, ancient crafts and original materials are increasingly difficult to find and costs of repair work rise faster than other costs. In addition, old buildings in private ownership are likely to attract high levels of estate and succession duties, capital transfer tax and income tax, and to cap all else, repairs are subject to value added tax. Land values, tax assessments and costs of maintenance are based on outdated, often unrealistically high, appraisals of the earning capacity of old buildings. To an investor they appear inefficient, unsafe, insanitary and uncomfortable, and many are situated in decaying inner-city areas.

The objectives of preservationists conflict with the financial and commercial interests of property owners. Many owners, including public bodies, neglect their legal obligations to protect historic monuments and a few deliberately destroy buildings that have become obsolete or stand in the way of profitable developments. The pulling down of Euston Arch, the wilful abandonment of the Grange in Hampshire, the smashing of the Art-Deco front of the Firestone factory are only the most notorious incidents to reach the attention of newspaper readers. Many scandalous acts of defiance are repeated furtively, away from the glare of publicity. In sleepy, untroubled neighbourhoods, thousands of churches, chapels, railway stations, cotton mills, country houses and medieval barns have been desecrated, mutilated and demolished.

Worse still, in my opinion, new buildings in the manner of Seifert and Lasdun are designed to disrupt the proportions of old streets, to block vistas, to break skylines, to open gaps in balanced frontages and systematically to attack the order and harmony of old quarters. This aggressive archi-tecture shuns the old as dirty, decrepit, decayed – a poor, unworthy neighbour to the gleaming new towers and mighty concrete blocks.

A history of revival, restoration and preservation suggests that historic landscapes will not be saved by a head-on clash between owners of old buildings and the law. If owners are discouraged from removing redundant parts of listed buildings, the law will be defied and the buildings themselves will fall. Insistence upon strict preservation must be relaxed to permit decaying quarters to be restored and adapted to new uses. In some places, a satisfying old-fashioned atmosphere may be evoked by building in revival styles, by incorporating period decoration, by retaining the ground plan, scale and proportions of old lanes, courts and façades. In other places, old buildings may be respectfully altered to serve new functions and to accommodate modern amenities. In the past, imagination, improvisation and adaptability saved the English landscape heritage. These qualities were never more needed than at present.

FURTHER READING

Evans, Joan. *A History of the Society of Antiquaries.* London: The Society of Antiquaries, 1956. Traces the development of relations between English antiquarians and preservationists.

Fawcett, Jane (ed.). *The Future of the Past: Attitudes to Conservation, 1174–1974.* London: Thames & Hudson for the Victorian Society, 1976. Essays by Pevsner, Betjeman, Osbert Lancaster and others discussing the architectural claims of buildings to be preserved, and the history of the preservation movement.

Henderson, Philip (ed.). *The Letters of William Morris to His Family and Friends.* London: Longmans, Green, 1950. Includes Morris's letter to the *Athenaeum,* 1877.

Hussey, Christopher. *The Picturesque: Studies in a Point of View.* London: Frank Cass, 1967. Sympathetic insights into eighteenth-century attitudes towards historical and mock-historical features in the English landscape.

Jones, Barbara. *Follies and Grottoes.* London: Constable, 1974. A delightfully illustrated guide to English follies with serious historical notes.

Munby, Lionel M. *The Hertfordshire Landscape.* London: Hodder & Stoughton, 1977. Contains Chauncy's eulogy of Ralph Freeman and many other memorable observations of Hertfordshire in the past.

Pevsner, Nikolaus. *Hertfordshire (The Buildings of England).* Harmondsworth: Penguin, 1953; 2nd ed., revised by Bridget Cherry, 1977. The indispensable inventory of buildings of architectural interest without which no account of revival, restoration or preservation would be complete.

Piggott, Stuart. *Ruins in a Landscape: Essays in Antiquarianism.* Edinburgh: University Press, 1976. Especially helpful on the origins and seventeenth-century history of antiquarianism and archaeology.

Strong, Roy. *The Renaissance Garden in England.* London: Thames & Hudson, 1979. Sheds fresh light on a largely forgotten phase of garden-making.

Summerson, John. *Architecture in Britain: 1530–1830.* 6th edition. Harmondsworth: Penguin, 1977. A profound and scholarly account of the history of buildings in Britain and the changes of taste that underlie architectural history.

Part II

WHAT WE TREASURE
AND WHY

PRESERVATION IS increasingly comprehensive. Ever more catholic about the buildings we choose to save, we also extend our concern to all manner of past remains. Historic preservation has concentrated on architectural features, but ancient buildings have never pre-empted interest in other antiquities. Portable religious relics and works of art have long been cherished no less for age than for spiritual and aesthetic merit.

Historical artifacts of every kind, if less well endowed or protected by legislation than our architectural heritage, now attract unparalleled attention. Recent exhibitions of Egyptian relics, Viking crafts, Inca gold, and the bygones of Pompeii have drawn record museum audiences. Auction sales of ancient masterpieces continually reach new heights; trifling antiques change hands for sums that would only recently have seemed astronomical.

The risks of theft and forgery that attend these inflated values parallel the erosion and demolition of the built environment. A flourishing black market in antiquities combined with the advanced technology available to treasure hunters make archaeological relics everywhere the prey of professional thieves and amateur adventurers alike. Widespread copying is another consequence of the high value and scarcity of genuine antiques. Growing sophistication in the detection of fraudulent antiquing has done little to stem this ancient practice. Nor is the fake past limited to forgeries: acknowledged imitations and replicas also proliferate. How far reproduction furniture and art works debase real antiquities is hotly disputed, but such

51

contrivances clearly affect the context of the surviving past.

The attrition and debasement of treasured relics is partly compensated for by the extension of historical value to an increasing range of commodities. Antiques are progressively more inclusive both in time — 1970s things already have historical value — and in content. A new encyclopedia describes scores of 'collectibles' which ten or twenty years ago would have been thrown away as junk, but today find an assured place both in popular history and in the hearts of collectors.

Like historic buildings, other surviving antiquities also have symbolic worth; they are felt to exemplify ancestral spirit and skills. In Britain, the sale of antiquities abroad occasions vehement protests about the loss of the national heritage; other lands, previously deprived of their artifactual and archival heritage, nowadays press through UNESCO for their return. Determining the rightful heirs to the Code of Hammurabi, now in the Louvre; deciding whether the Leonardo Leicester Codex was part of the British heritage; weighing the perils of loss and erosion against Nigerian claims for the return of Benin bronzes from the British Museum — these typify the problems aroused by the removal of antiquities at least since Lord Elgin stole (or saved) the Parthenon sculptures.

These several realms of our heritage interconnect. An historic house and park furnished with inherited antiques and family portraits and memorabilia conveys immeasurably more of the past than would each item in museumized isolation. But scarcity, fashion and politics often impel us to concentrate on one aspect of the material heritage to the exclusion or neglect of others. Lands lacking a lengthy architectural heritage must make do with portable relics, or vice versa. Bereft of almost all other antiquities and art treasures, Poland was the more fiercely determined to restore its war-destroyed medieval city centres. In Britain, tax-beleaguered historic-house owners often sell off antiques or art works to enable them to keep intact the basic fabric of the house itself.

Different sorts of people treasure different pieces of the past. Those attached to historic buildings of any vintage, whether medieval, Georgian, Victorian or Art Deco, all share a common background — a background quite unlike that of the steam-railway buff. The bottle-cap fanatic, the earthwork enthusiast, the Georgian silver devotee each represent different preservation constituencies, apt to have more in common from country to country than from commodity to commodity.

The chapters in Part II tackle questions as various as the aspects of our heritage they concern. Peter J. Fowler is concerned with the prehistoric past on at least three counts: that it should be professionally interpreted, that it should provide public interest and enjoyment, and that it should be safeguarded for future archaeological study. These concerns converge in his downgrading of excavation in favour of aerial photography and other modes of examination which enable professional archaeologists to study materials without disturbing them, allow the public to enjoy undespoiled sites, and leave evidence intact for better-equipped scholars of the future.

Fowler also seeks to bridge the gulf between professionals and the public, which must ultimately pay for archaeological study. The remote past holds immense appeal both in Europe, where ancient man is a link with our own early heritage, and in America, where the primordial indigene seems a wholly exotic figure; on both continents, thousands annually volunteer for digs and other archaeological work. Most popular interest in prehistory focuses on death and treasure, however, ignoring the humdrum, everyday aspects of archaeological analysis. Moreover, professional arch-aeologists tend to scoff at public fascination with the occult, such as black magic and ley lines.

With antiques we are in a wholly different world, and Bevis Hillier conducts us on a journey unlike any other in this volume. He explores the passion for antiques as seen by poets and essayists fascinated with collectors' obsessions. But beyond avarice and absurdities, antiques serve as fetishes for conjuring up the past, reassuringly tangible emanations that are often more serviceable than old houses because they are portable, require little maintenance, and seldom infringe on the view. At the same time, an interest in antiques often leads to an appreciation of the historical environments in which they were originally used, and so to preservation in the broader sense.

Landscapes, wholly unlike antiques, are historical remains that figure in everybody's view. Less consciously selected for preservation than buildings or other artifacts, landscape features also flow into one another in a fashion that obscures their historical pedigrees. Differences of scale, lack of visual distinctiveness, and difficulty of dating with precision make landscapes hard to define as antiquities and also hard to preserve, as Marion Shoard shows. And because landscapes are aggregations of growing things that continually replenish themselves, we have difficulty in imagining that they can ever be wholly 'lost'.

Yet there are powerful arguments for preserving landscape features, even entire landscapes. Ancient hedgerows, open-field relics, and other historic traces are as consequential as, and often far more evocative than, any built structures. Observation and activity from childhood on connect us fundamentally with our landscape inheritance. The consequences of man's interaction with natural processes, as uniquely embodied in historic landscapes, engender profound and perhaps essential attachments to locale.

Yet despite the evident appreciation of millions of visitors, native and foreign, landscape preservation in England is in a desperate plight. Not only are landscape benefits harder to quantify than other aspects of our material heritage, but powerful entrenched interests, notably forestry and farming, generally oppose their conservation. The motives and machinery that make the agricultural industry the main threat to landscape preservation confound the rural nostalgia that sees farmers as stewards of the landscape. Specifically and exclusively exempt from ordinary planning controls, farmers regularly receive grants for destroying historic landscape features in the misconceived aim of agricultural self-sufficiency. By contrast, rural sentiment in some favoured areas that are marginal to agriculture, together with back-to-nature life-styles, allows Americans to perceive family farming as the bedrock of landscape preservation.

Tamara Hareven and Randolph Langenbach show how the developing concern with industrial archaeology has begun to alter the entire idea of preservation. Who until now would have considered preserving New England factory towns and Lancashire textile mills? Some have appreciated these structures for their aesthetic majesty, but until recently the usual response on both sides of the Atlantic was total lack of interest in, if not outright condemnation of, the seamier relics of the Industrial Revolution. Now it is clear that such buildings matter not only to architects and historians, but still more to those who have lived and worked in them, and to the communities whose heritage they are. Even those who found life in these places hard and dour have kept an affection for them as ingredients of their everyday lives: familiar scenes that may not be endearing, but that nonetheless incarnate essential memories.

Local interest in such industrial complexes shows how preservation, like history itself, increasingly concerns things not because they were special but because they were ordinary, not because they were exotic but because they were homely. Like the family photographs and seaside souvenirs on our mantels, the homes and workplaces of yesteryear keep their value for those who inhabited them, a value that is confirmed by their endurance into the present.

CHAPTER 3

Archaeology, the Public and the Sense of the Past

PETER J. FOWLER

ARCHAEOLOGY MEANS, literally, a knowledge of old things. Today, more properly, it is the acquisition of more and better information about the past, the use of that information to develop a better understanding of the past, and the dissemination of both information and understanding to the world of scholarship and the public. 'Old' starts yesterday, and indeed I often find myself today looking at the present and identifying what is going to be the archaeology of tomorrow. One weekend I photographed a wooden-clad signal station in anticipation of its redundancy when the Bedford–St Pancras railway goes all-electric in 1982; the next I learnt that it had just been listed as a building of historical interest, so I am not alone in my thoughts.

The essence of archaeology is its approach to a past primarily by way of surviving material culture. Absolute age is irrelevant to this approach except that archaeology is the only approach for 99 per cent of human history. Otherwise, that approach is as valid for the most recent two thousand years as for the previous two million, and it matters not whether the evidence is below or above ground level.

The public in this context is first of all that minority which is consciously interested in the past as represented by what archaeology studies and produces. This minority ranges from the few hundred people, in Britain anyway, engaged at levels ranging from that of manual drudgery to academic theorizing, to the hundreds of thousands who knowingly devote part of their time to archaeological matters. Beyond this are two bands of the population. The inner consists of several million people who have some awareness of and perhaps a mild interest in the past. The outer, much broader band comprises the bulk of the population who, frankly, do not give a damn about the past or archaeology. Their ignorance, however, does not vitiate their need of both at a communal if not an individual level.

'The sense of the past' is a knowingly ambiguous phrase, and I shall touch on only three of its meanings. Academics, educationalists, sociologists and politicians all use the phrase, albeit for different reasons. In general, they mean that communities (though not necessarily all the individuals in them) are aware of the past as a function of time and as a collective experience. A conscious if ill-defined awareness of this past is part of their intellectual environment. In this sense, the past is quite specifically *not* merely something which *has* happened: a sense of the past is by definition a contemporary phenomenon. It is there even if passive; more often, when invoked, it is an active factor influencing current thought, and therefore perpetuating that influence into the future.

As an archaeologist, the meaning of the phrase 'the sense of the past' I more frequently come across is that of the past making sense to us as we peer back at it. Even in this limited context there are at least two levels of meaning. First, does the past make sense to us in that *we* can reasonably reconstruct what happened and why? And second, does what we perceive to be the past itself make sense in that events or people appear to have happened or acted in an explicable, rational manner, by their terms of reference and/or by ours?

I shall explore these meanings of 'sense of the past' a little further. My main concern, however, is the relationships among the three elements of my title. The truism from which I start is that the past is a much more organic and complex phenomenon than might be suggested by frenetic local attempts to prop up an old building or those television clichés of serious-faced students scratching the soil with a mason's trowel in the name of archaeology.

Archaeology and its past

What archaeology does, and the way it does it, is very much constrained by the way the discipline has developed. What it has done at any time in its past — and here we are talking of no more than four centuries — has been very much a reflection of contemporary life, both sociologically and intellectually. Far from being an irrelevance on the pale of society, archaeology is a very sensitive indicator indeed of changes in social attitudes and in the elements of society itself. By and large, society gets the archaeology is deserves; it is next to impossible for archaeology to dictate its own terms or to break free of social constraints. It is these general constraints which have placed archaeology in such a richly frustrating state of tension today.

What the modern archaeologist is trying to do academically seems reasonably clear and rational to those involved; but it is in practice difficult to convey to the public at large. So here straight away are two tensions: that within the discipline between traditional concerns and relatively progressive outlooks; and that between what many archaeologists are seeking to do now and what society expects them to be doing. The tensions are certainly not unique to archaeology — a glance at biology in the 1860s and geography in the 1960s tells us that. Archaeology today nevertheless has two distinct pasts to cope with — the past of its own history and the past which it is in business to study. The idea that it is also in business to preserve the latter past has for long been an element in archaeological thought — witness John Aubrey in the seventeenth century and the fact that we are approaching the centenary of the first Ancient Monuments Act in Britain. But only in the most recent decade has preservation come to be generally recognized amongst archaeologists themselves as one of their major priorities.

The immediate occasion for this growing awareness is quite simply the intensification of archaeological destruction, a trend especially marked in the 1960s. Not only could existing resources not cope with the rate of destruction — as is still the case — but archaeologists whose main interests were in museum study or in teaching found that, in the field, their discipline had quite suddenly become so ravaged that whole classes of site were now limited to a few surviving examples or were perhaps extinct altogether. Furthermore, whole palaeo-landscapes providing the cultural context within which conventional archaeological sites existed were also being extensively obliterated. The recognition of these facts reflected a stage in the intellectual development of the subject as much as what could be seen in the landscape. Such recognition extended the preservation problem horizontally when previously it had been one mainly of a free-standing site and the ground beneath it.

Archaeology needs deliberate preservation of some sites and landscapes for several reasons, but let us be quite specific about the main one. It is no less absolutely justified because it is selfish, introspective and based on such an unfashionable matter as scholarship. Whatever else is done in the name of archaeology, the subject itself is basically an academic discipline, a scholarly pursuit based upon the informed study of the cultural products of the past. In this respect, when it meets with other interests on the common ground of preservation, conservation or amenity, it is not a meeting of like with like, except in relation to that common interest; whatever may be the nature of rambling and pony trekking, for example, it does not derive from an academic base. Such interests demand conservation primarily for people; archaeology needs preservation primarily for itself so that it may continue to develop scholastically. One of the results of preservation may well be to enhance understanding through further research, and in that way benefit people, but unless the subject actually has the material on which to work it will fossilize and benefit no one. And ultimately that material is in the field.

Obviously we cannot sterilize the whole landscape for academic research. Many sites are already protected; museums are bulging with unstudied and unpublished material anyway. Such points, however, overlook the dynamic relationship between archaeology and its past. The discipline needs a constant supply of new data and, although destruction ensures that there is no shortage of them at the moment, we must consciously build those reservoirs of potential information for the archaeological research of the twenty-first century and beyond. Archaeology is not merely knowledge of the past; it is also the safeguarding of the future study of the past. By what we preserve now we of course affect the nature of future research, but that is the least of our problems. We cannot anticipate what the future is going to want to know about its past — which will include us. What we can do, granted our recognition that the past will have a role to play in the future, is to select and set aside some of our past in the hope that our successors will find at least some of it useful for their purposes tomorrow.

What sort of archaeology are we preserving for the future? Generally, the material falls into three classes. First, those sites and buildings which are consciously given a new lease of life as 'show-piece archaeology', the display sites made safe, probably restored or reconstructed, and made available to the public. The state's role here is represented by 'Guardianship' monuments, but there are many other arrangements for this type of preservation by other bodies. With display the priority, the selection of sites for such treatment is biased towards the visually impressive and the stone-built, neither of which characteristics necessarily correlates with archaeological significance. Most prehistoric building in Britain, for example, was in wood which has not survived. Furthermore, the treatment of such sites, and the subsequent access to them by perhaps millions of feet over a period of years, may well not be in the best interests of those sites from an academic point of view. Even if they have been properly excavated

restoration

first, by definition they will have been largely destroyed, because modern excavation of a site is a non-repeatable exercise in total resource exploitation. So here is a marvellous 'Catch-22' situation: such preservation usually in fact means damage and sometimes destruction. Subsequent care and maintenance where this has happened could well be of a modern piece of quasi-heritage, impressive maybe for the public but a monumental dodo from an academic point of view. Not for arch for public IRestoration

Second, those parts of our heritage which have been designated in one way or another — in England, listed if a building is in use, scheduled if an Ancient Monument — but to which the public have no consequential rights of access. For administrative, political and financial reasons, there are many more of these than there are maintained sites – *c*. 275,000 listed buildings and *c*. 12,000 scheduled monuments, for example. This group therefore represents a larger sample of the cultural heritage, but it has not been compiled on criteria other than of 'national importance'. It is still not a scientific sample. It is understandably biased towards individual sites rather than areas of cultural landscape, towards the upstanding rather than the flat (whereas most of the archaeological heritage *is* already flat), towards that which is on Ordnance Survey maps rather than to that which is archaeologically significant. In practice, too, scheduling has proved to be inadequate as a preserving mechanism; many thousands of archaeological sites so designated have in fact been damaged or even destroyed. Nevertheless, and particularly in the light of the new for Arch Ancient Monuments and Archaeological Areas Act (April 1979), the Schedule of Ancient Monuments overall represents a more significant academic reservoir of archaeological potential than the Guardianship sites.

Third, that part of the archaeological heritage which has been accidentally protected — perhaps we should say non-specifically protected. Without there being any official national policy, sites and, more importantly, chunks of cultural landscape happen to have been included in areas defined and set aside for special but non-archaeological functions. In this category come principally National Parks, the land-holdings of the National Trust, national and local Nature Reserves in the countryside, and Conservation Areas in towns and villages. Such areas are of unequal importance archaeologically, but all are of actual or potential significance primarily because they involve areas, tracts of countryside; and it is primarily landscapes, urban and rural, not discrete sites, that archaeology as an academic discipline needs now and in future. Neither sites nor their peoples ever existed in a vacuum. Archaeology therefore needs space to promote more accurate understanding of the past. A generation ago it was recognized that the study of that past must concern itself with people, not just things; if our concerns have now moved on to the study of relationships, just as much of current geography seems to be involved with chaps as well as maps, so archaeology's chaps increasingly express themselves horizontally through maps in addition to the time-depth of stratification. The horizontal dimension is essential for future study of the past.

From archaeology's point of view, then, there is one overriding, scholarly reason for preserving a representative sample of its source material in the field. 'Whither archaeology?' will become 'wither archaeology' without that. But of course there are other, non-academic, reasons for saving parts of our common cultural past. They could well be as important as the purist, academic one.

The public and its past

In relation to its past, that amorphous creature, the public, exists at minimally three levels of awareness, as described above. The first, that of the committed minority, is influential among the even smaller number of professionals. There are, however, tensions. Is it, for example, the role of the committed to further archaeology or to use it to release their desk-bound frustrations at the weekend? The sociology of involvement in contemporary archaeology is an as yet unexplored field; but whatever the motivation, the amateur contribution to archaeology has been enormous, and it still has a significant part to play in an increasingly professional and complex field. Archaeology must not lose its vital support from the 'committed public'.

Numerically, archaeology's greatest support is from the segment of the public which is casually interested, generally aware, but not actively involved. Essentially it is the bulk of the television audience, the visitors to museums, and the tourists at the 'display sites'. If we knew exactly what they wanted, TV programmes, museums, and site displays could doubtless be improved; but the public expectation is not always what archaeology is about or is capable of producing. Unless it is dauntingly labelled 'Education', for example, TV archaeology must primarily entertain, yet archaeology in its 'natural' state is not necessarily entertaining. In fact, much of its work, perhaps particularly on excavations, is repetitive, routine and visually boring, and much of its surviving field material, even earthworks, is flatly unphotogenic. And because the bulk of that material is already invisible, or at best pinned two-dimensionally to an air photograph, we are largely reduced for our visual, tangible history to museum objects which in themselves no longer represent the main thrust of archaeological research.

There is then a potential, and often a real, gap between archaeology as expected on the one hand, and archaeology as it really is on the other. This is not unique to archaeology, of course, and the difficulties of bridging the gap are no excuse for not trying to do so; but to a certain extent the subject is forced to conform to the stereotype of expectation. That public expectation is centred around death and treasure. Neither is particularly germane to much archaeology in the field, and of course neither is likely to be encountered anyway if the emphasis is on preservation rather than excavation. So there is a dichotomy, increasing in my view, between archaeology doing what is right by its own criteria and producing what its public expects it to

produce, indeed sees as its *raison d'être*. It is difficult enough
to put over the doctrine of 'cultural resource management'
within the profession; a course of action stemming from
the premise that the prime objective is to perpetuate for as
long as possible the life of the resource – in this case
archaeological landscape phenomena – will neither bring
the annual Fossick Award of the Little Gidding Excavation
Club nor set the ratings all a-quiver in Granada-land.

No assumptions can be made about keeping the interest
of the more general public. Yet, if archaeology is to
proceed at all other than as an introverted specialism for
the recondite few, the retention and indeed the development
of the public interest is vital. Ultimately, the public pays
the piper and its right to influence the tune has to be
accepted. Better, so the argument runs, for the feet to wear
out a few sites in the expression of public interest than for
the public to vote with its feet by not visiting at all. So,
despite my earlier 'purist' case for the need to preserve for
archaeology's own sake, clearly what we preserve, how we
preserve it and to what end, invokes a complex situation in
which losses, disappointments and mistakes are as inevitable
as is compromise. Successes now and, more importantly,
future assessment that our action was successful, depend to
a large extent on the strength of 'the sense of the past'.

The sense of the past

The past may not always make much sense to us, but we
feel that it ought to. It has to make sense of a sort for we are
its product; it would demean our self-respect if we had just
happened rather than been the result of rational or at least
explicable processes. Even so, an explanation of the past
does not have to be scientific to be appealing; indeed the
reverse may be the case. One of modern archaeology's
weaknesses is that its version of what happened, particularly
for prehistoric times, is for many people less satisfactory
than *deus ex machina* explanations. The latter have an instant
simplicity of cause and effect, appealing on the one hand to

the modern cult of technology with bionic space ships, and on the other to the age-old cult of mysteriousness with its dark forces, straight lines and a complete disregard for scholarship. Archaeologists may dismiss such theories for the fantasies that they are, but they are not helped by the half-baked dabblings of scholars from other disciplines who lend a spurious respectability to the quest of the irrational; but such dismissal does not alter the failure of mainstream archaeology to produce a coherent image of the past for today. Meanwhile, the versions other than those of academic archaeology are much more attractive to many lay people who, however obscurely, need to have with them a past in the present. The most important criterion of a past may indeed be that it should 'speak' to the proverbial man in the street. If so, then the past is not an absolute quantity but a relative set of values. Such indeed would seem to be the case if we look at the acceptable pasts portrayed in European literature and art over the last two hundred years. In a sense, then, my pleas as an academic for the needs of scholarship to be recognized as the basis for preservation policies may well be irrelevant (though I do not believe so). It is an assumption of cultural research nevertheless that it will reveal a pattern from which explanation will stem; but what if research reveals chaos or nothingness, an aimless blundering through the sands of time? Surely it is because of the failure of conventional research to allay that fear altogether, that a Garden of Eden syndrome is, psychologically if not intellectually, still well-received even in this age of educated enlightenment. The cave-man's perception of a past still lurks beneath the *New Scientist* veneer of rationality; scratch a 'Guardian' reader and she is more likely to be swinging a pendulum over a plan of the Cerne Giant than poring through the *Proceedings of the Prehistoric Society*.

Writers figure prominently among those most overtly affected by the memorials of times past. They have frequently referred to the same few characteristics of the past. Above all, they evoke its power to stimulate the human imagination. Thoughts of wonder, sadness, faded grandeur, their own insignificance, mortality and solitariness are the small change of topographical currency, as subjective pens have scribbled about emotions we can probably now best experience on a bank holiday in the commercial centres of our inner city deserts. Perhaps thereby is a moral. We certainly will not be so stimulated at the display sites on holidays as Mr General Public queues his way through the Tower or inches round the Stonehenge circuit. All the same, the financial implications of modern tourism now provide a whole new set of criteria for what we should preserve and why, which have very little to do with romantic antiquarian musings or scientific archaeological enquiry.

The visible, tangible past may be culture but it is now very much money too. Not only do its attractions make a measurable contribution to national incomes, as in Britain and Greece; at numerous places, the whole of a local economy is very much dependent on it. And such is the level of visitor interest at the moment that new 'archaeological monuments' are being constructed: for charitable and research purposes as at the Butser 'Ancient Farm' in Hampshire; for entertainment as with the BBC's 'Iron-Age Village' built to make television programmes; and for commercial purposes as at several other perhaps less valid reconstructions. The idea behind the national folk museums with their genuine material, long established at St Fagan's and in Oslo, for example, is being developed in regional counterparts such as the Weald and Downland Museum in Sussex and the open-air museum at Beamish, Co. Durham, and imitated in numerous local and thematic presentations. Indeed, the conventional archaeological display site, such as a castle or stone circle, now has many competitors: several agricultural museums dealing with material and processes of the last hundred years, for example, have recently appeared on the scene, in part, I suspect, reflecting the popular successes of rural traction-engine rallies.

Prehistory can barely compete with this sort of phenomenon: hill forts do not puff and hoot and grandfather did not build stone circles as a boy. Psychologically, the communal recent past has a different sort of appeal from the remote past: its comprehensibility more than offsets its lack of mystery. For many, it is probably true that a sense of the past does not extend in any meaningful way further back than two or three generations to the beginnings of our contemporary world with electricity, the internal combustion engine, and the replacement of people and animals as sources of power by machines. Contemporary enthusiasms for and cults of a past of sorts may nevertheless mask a basic failure of the 'scholastic past' to advance at popular level what may well be its single most important contribution to society. That contribution is a sense of *perspective* in time. As a father of three schoolchildren myself, I am tempted to add that the way history is taught nowadays seems to contribute significantly to this failure: glittering pearls of Romans, cave-men, the battles of the First World War, medieval monks, and Stonehenge, suspended in temporal, non-causative isolation, hardly enhance appreciation of the necklace of time. Indeed, I sometimes suspect that in our temporal perception we are nearer to *1066 and All That* now than were my children's grandparents as children.

The past is thus much more than what has happened, much more than that which happens to have survived. We create the past of our own time merely by being; we fashion for ourselves that which we regard as the past; and we pre-empt in some degree that past of the future by what we preserve and by what we destroy now. Those who talk of the past as 'dead' fail to recognize its organic nature and to appreciate that, despite its physical existence as monuments and muniments, essentially it lives in the mind. That may seem strange coming from an archaeologist whose prime concern is professionally with what we can see and touch, measure and analyse, draw and photograph. But the objective data from such exercises are inert until they pass through my mind, the minds of colleagues and the minds of countless individuals, all of us forming society. These several pasts, like the poor, are always with us; and what we regard as worth keeping, and our reasons for so thinking, must therefore be relative, changing with people, with time, with fashion and with research – and with what is left to preserve. Physically, the past is not an inexhaustible resource; managerially, it has to be viewed as a finite resource. The extent to which our generation has depleted the archaeological resource in Britain is on such a scale as permanently to affect the future's vision of the past. Indeed, our behaviour in the mid-twentieth century is now permanently reflected in our treatment of what we inherited as our past. We shall inevitably be judged in part by what we now pass on; by our criteria, never mind the future's, the judgement must be deservedly harsh.

My conclusion must be, granted the relative nature of the past, that it is imperative for its custodians, self-appointed or official, to be not backward-looking, not even men of their own time. The real challenge to the 'old fogeys' concerned about the past is to break free of their contemporary social constraints and to be conceptually ahead of their time. A sense of the past may require an intellectually sophisticated frame of mind; to anticipate what that sense will require in the future is even more demanding. And if sceptics concerned only with the present demand a practical reason for the attempt, the justification surely is that nothing could be more an expression of human hope for the future than trying to give it something for its past. After all, if there is no future, then it will need no past. Why we want to pass on some of our inheritance is because we believe *Homo sapiens* has a future, and because in that future he will need a past. In a curious but exciting way, our anticipation of a future need of a past with reference points supplied by us is one of the few ways in which a dialogue can be developed with posterity. Our successors may not like what we offer, they will doubtless interpret it differently, but, in reacting, they will at least have something on which to exercise that most idiosyncratic asset of *Homo sapiens*, the human mind.

FURTHER READING

Clark, Grahame. *Archaeology and Society: Reconstructing the Prehistoric Past*. London: Methuen, 1939; University Paperback, 1960. One of the few studies by a prehistorian of the relationships between modern society and its material past.

Crawford, O. G. S. *Man and His Past*. London: Oxford University Press, 1921. Captures a time when realization was dawning that archaeology was more than digging up things in isolation. Now mainly of historic interest.

Darvill, J. C., *et al* (eds). *New Approaches to Our Past: An Archaeological Forum*. Southampton: University of Southampton Archaeological Society, 1978. An interesting, if not entirely successful, attempt to point the way forward just as the 'Rescue archaeology' bubble of the 1970s was beginning to burst.

Fowler, Peter J. *Approaches to Archaeology*. London: Adam and Charles Black, 1977. Relates conventional archaeology to the many changes in studies of and attitudes towards the past in the 1970s.

McGimsey, C. R., and Davis, H. A. (eds). *The Management of Archeological Resources*. Washington, D.C.: Special Publication of the Society for American Archeology, 1977. A symposium, influential in Britain, reflecting American archaeologists' intellectual and practical efforts to come to grips with 'public archaeology'.

Newcomb, Robert M. *Planning the Past: Historical Landscape Resources and Recreation*. Folkestone, Kent: Dawson; and Hamden, Conn.: Archon Books/The Shoe String Press, 1979. Not a contradiction but a sensible and wide-ranging discussion of how the past is, and could be, looked after.

Rahtz, Philip A. (ed.). *Rescue Archaeology*. Harmondsworth: Penguin, 1974. Dated on publication, but still the only popular presentation on what was and is happening to Britain's archaeological heritage.

Rowley, R. T., and Breakall, Mike (eds). *Planning and the Historic Environment* I, II. Department for External Studies, University of Oxford, 1975, 1977. Archaeologists' concerns and practices in the rapidly changing cultural landscape of Britain; the British equivalent to McGimsey and Davis, above.

Schiffer, Michael B., and Gumerman, George J. (eds). *Conservation Archeology: A Guide for Cultural Resource Management Studies*. New York and London: Academic Press, 1977. Elaborate and sophisticated American expression of concern about cultural resource management.

Shoard, Marion. *The Theft of the Countryside*. London: Maurice Temple Smith, 1980. Dynamite; rural Britain's equivalent of Rachel Carson's *Silent Spring*.

CHAPTER 4

Why Do We Collect Antiques?

BEVIS HILLIER

SOME TIME ago I wrote an editorial in *The Connoisseur* suggesting that we needed a Minister of Conservation. I began by asking readers to imagine themselves in Sotheby's or Christie's when a Chelsea porcelain teapot of the eighteenth century was being sold. What, I asked, would be their reaction if, immediately the teapot was sold for, say, £4,000, the man who had bought it came up to the rostrum with a hammer and smashed the teapot to smithereens? Naturally they would be amazed and horrified and would feel that the man should be carted off to an asylum as soon as possible. Of course the man would have the legal right to do as he pleased with his own property though he might be arrested for conduct likely to cause a breach of the peace.

It is not hard to guess the point I was trying to bring home with this shocking image. It was that every day, in Britain, far more appalling destruction is taking place – the destruction, by *their* owners, of unique and irreplaceable buildings of the past, of which even the commercial value (to use the only language the destroyers understand) is far greater than that of a Chelsea teapot. And no one is carted off to the lunatic asylum; no one is arrested for conduct likely to cause a breach of the peace.

Why is it that people are prepared to accept the violence done to great mansions worth upwards of £100,000 when they would protest vehemently at the smallest damage inflicted on a £4,000 teapot? Well, first, of course, the architectural destroyers do usually have some spurious 'justification' for their action: that a building is structurally unsafe and it would cost too much to repair it, or that its site is needed for a new block of flats or motorway – while it is hard to think of a good reason for 'redeveloping' a Chelsea teapot. But I think there is more to it than that. If one accepts, as I do, that one of the main purposes of studying our history is to help us put ourselves in our right context (for without a knowledge of history we would all be like babies left in baskets on doorsteps, not knowing whence we came) then antiques are the reassuring, tangible fragments of that past: like the scale from a fairy's wing or the golden apple from a magical banquet that the child is still left clutching after his adventures in fairy-tales, to convince him that it wasn't all just a dream. If we did not dig up coins and statues of Roman emperors, it would be difficult to give credence to anything Gibbon tells us. An embroidery worked by Mary Queen of Scots during her imprisonment helps to persuade us that Lady Antonia Fraser's *Life* of that queen is not just a romance.

So my own interest in antiques is as talismans, fetish-objects for conjuring up the past; the antique collector is an archaeologist without a spade. But, at the same time, I cannot claim to be, except in the most desultory way, an antique *collector*. The motives which impel antique collectors on their sometimes obsessional courses are quite different. They may be indulging their aesthetic tastes and surrounding themselves with fatty deposits of buhl and ormolu. They may be enjoying the detective work of making up *sets* of things, in the manner of the stamp collector. They may be financially avaricious and looking for a hedge against inflation. And sometimes there seems to be no sane motive for their activities – one thinks of the American collector described by Ambrose Bierce, who collected champagne corks and recorded in a book the dates of their several poppings; or the bizarre hoarder described in these lines by Alistair Sampson (who himself, incidentally, sells antiques in the Brompton Road):

> Today I had a big surprise,
> Uncle left me eight glass eyes.
> He never used the things himself –
> He kept them glaring on a shelf.

And champing on the shelf beneath
Were twenty-seven sets of teeth.
He always was the life and soul
Of every party. He would roll
An eye along the floor and shout:
'Archie, yours has fallen out.'
Uncle's eyes were funny hues,
Mottled greens and pretty blues.
The one he slipped in people's drink
Was flecked with palest, palest pink . . . .

What is it that makes people collect? It is a question that has been much pecked over; and quoting those lines of modern verse suggests to me an original and perhaps rewarding way of tackling it – by drawing on the entire resources of British verse for references to antique collecting and seeing what themes emerge. Poets have something in common with collectors. Both assemble images, whether physical or metaphorical, and arrange them in sequences: the collector on shelves, the poet in lines. Both the choice and the arrangement of images are at the despotic discretion of poet or collector – a power that would be absolute but for limitations of mind or purse respectively.

The first English poem that I have been able to find which describes a collector is Alexander Barclay's translation of Brandt's *Ship of Fools*, printed by Wynkyn de Worde in 1508. These lines are a satire on a medieval bibliomane:

I am the first fool of the whole navie
To keep the poupe, the helme, and eke the sayle:
For this is my minde, this one pleasure have I,
Of bookes to have great plentie and apparayle.
Still I am busy bookes assembling,
For to have plenty it is a pleasant thing
In my conceyt, and to have them aye in hande:
But what they meane do I not understande.
But yet I have them in great reverence
And honoure, saving them from filth and ordure,
By often brushing and much diligence;

72

Ful goodly bound in pleasaunt coverture,
Of damas, satten, or else of velvet pure....

Here, then, is that recurring figure of fun, the collector
who collects for show, or because it is the fashion, and has
no understanding of the antiques in his collection. We all
know them; and I suspect they are the most frequent breed
of all – yet let us not condemn them out-of-hand. At least
they do preserve the antiques, and feel some pathetic
reverence for them, of the kind the proverbial cannibal
may feel when a wristwatch is washed up on the beach of his
desert island. Two centuries after the book collector was
satirized in *The Ship of Fools*, Pope was making exactly the
same joke about the Earl of Burlington:

His study! with what authors is it stored?
In books, not authors, curious is my Lord;
To all their dated backs he turns you round;
These Aldus printed, those Du Sueil has bound.
Lo, some are vellum, and the rest as good,
For all his Lordship knows, but they are wood.

James Bramston gives much the same impression of a
picture collector in *The Man of Taste* (1733):

In curious paintings I'm exceeding nice,
And know their several beauties by their price.
Auctions and sales I constantly attend,
But chuse my pictures by a skilful friend.
Originals and copies much the same,
The picture's value is the painter's name.

The undiscriminating collector, with his hoard of miscel-
laneous junk, is also ridiculed. He is the man who collects
in the same way as the ninth-century Welshman Nennius
wrote history. '*Coacervavi*,' said Nennius, '*omne quod inveni*' – I
have made a heap of all that I have found. A perfect
example of the Nennian method of collecting is George
Colman's Ozias Polyglot:

In every bedroom there were placed
Knick-knackeries of wondrous taste,
With shells and spars, stuffed birds, and flies
    in amber;
And by the side of every bed
There stood a Grecian urn instead
Of what is called in France a *pot-de-chambre*.

But if the poets are harsh on the collector who puts his collection above the things collected, they are merciless to him whose love for his collection exceeds, or is a substitute for, love of his fellow humans. Austin Dobson (who was actually an ardent collector himself) wrote a poem called 'A Virtuoso' which describes a visit to a collector by a representative of a deserving charity, war victims. The miserly old collector shows the visitor his oil paintings of tragic war scenes but ends by refusing the appeal. As the guest leaves, the collector shows him a Dürer figure of 'Charity' for which he has just paid £300.

Earlier, in 1725, John Gay had described a lady so besotted with old china that her suitors despair:

What ecstasies her bosom fire!
How her eyes languish with desire!
How blest, how happy I should be,
Were that fond glance bestow'd on me!
New doubts and fear within me war:
What rival's near? A china jar.

The collector as dupe (and we know him too) is made to seem as unengaging as the collector who is a cunning, avaricious exploiter. To Pope, Sir Andrew Fountaine was 'False as his gems and cancer'd as his Coins'. The Irish peasants of John Stevenson's 'The Antiquary' snigger at the old stones and rusty buckles that the visiting scholar is so eager to find. A. D. Godley (better known as the author of 'The Motor Bus'; 'What is it that roareth thus?') gets his own back on antique creation by mocking as 'paltry rubbish' a graven image that seems to be giving itself airs

and graces. Sir William Hamilton, the *mari complaisant* of
Nelson's Emma, is jocularly accused of faking his Etruscan
antiquities and baking them himself. A collector described
in another of Alistair Sampson's verses pays ten shillings
for a vase at a church bazaar:

> 'Ten bob,' she said, and blew a kiss.
> 'The Vicar will be told of this.'
> 'Will he?' I said, and left the grounds.
> The vase is worth five hundred pounds.

Naturally, dealers and auctioneers get their share of
odium from the poets. Every collector will be familiar with
the kind of dealer portrayed in Sampson's poem 'Fender',
who sings the praises of antique fenders until he finds that
the man who has come into his shop actually has one to *sell*.

The degradation of cherished possessions when they are
put up for auction is the subject of more than one poem.
The earliest treatment of the theme is by Thomas Otway:

> I passed this very moment by thy doors,
> And found them guarded by a troop of villains;
> The sons of public rapine were destroying,
> They told me, by the sentence of the law.
> They had commission to seize all thy fortune.
> Here stood a ruffian with a horrid face,
> Lording it o'er a heap of massive plate,
> Tumbled into a heap for public sale;
> There was another making villainous jests
> At thy undoing; he had ta'en possession
> Of all thy ancient, most domestic ornaments,
> Thy very bed was violated
> By the coarse hands of filthy dungeon slaves,
> And thrown amidst the common lumber!

These lines could well be an accurate description of the
sale-of-contents of Oscar Wilde's Tite Street house after
his trial in 1895, a scene evoked in all its cruelty by William
Gaunt in *The Aesthetic Adventure* (1945):

2 'The vase is worth five hundred pounds'
—Alistair Sampson

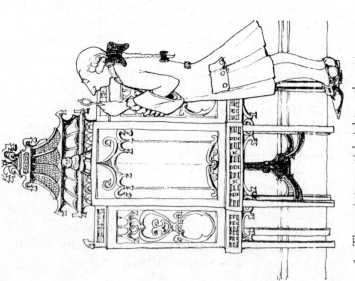

1 The quintessential eighteenth-century
antiques collector

The artist who had been rash enough to try conclusions with society was sold up. An inquisitive, careless rabble tramped through the rooms, and there was scarcely an appearance of order about the sale. Yet again, a collection of 'blue and white' was dispersed. Whistlers went for a pound or two. Letters and manuscripts disappeared without trace. In this way the Philistines took a disgraceful advantage of their enemy's fall.

Ironically, Wilde had himself written a (not very good) poem on the sale by auction of Keats's love-letters, somewhat melodramatically comparing this act with the dice-throwing for Christ's garments. The same kind of idea is expressed less apocalyptically in C. Day Lewis's poem 'Lot 96', about an iron fender which in the saleroom reflects 'not a ghost of the lives that illumed it':

> This lot was part of their precious bond, almost
> A property of its meaning. Here, in the litter
> Washed up by his death, values are re-assessed
> At a nod from the highest bidder.

This brings us straight back to the idea of the antique as a fetish-object which has soaked up some of the history to which it is a witness, and can help us to evoke that past (a function somehow nullified by the auction-room, just as a human being is impersonalized when up for sale in the slave market). In its least complicated form, the idea is responsible for many poems of the 'What changes you must have seen!' kind. My favourite among these is Horace Smith's 'Address to the Mummy in Belzoni's Exhibition', which after all is an antique of a kind:

> Did'st thou not hear the pother o'er thy head
> When the great Persian conqueror, Cambyses,
> Marched armies o'er thy tomb with thundering
>   tread,
> O'erthrew Osiris, Orus, Apis, Isis?
> And shook the pyramids with fear and wonder
> When the gigantic Memnon fell asunder?

If the tomb's secrets may not be confessed,

> The nature of thy private life unfold;
> A heart has throbbed beneath that leathern breast,
> And tears adown that dusky cheek have rolled.
> Have children climbed those knees and kissed that
>   face?
> What was thy name and station, age, and race?

The idea inspires more profound thoughts in poets of today. Anthony Thwaite (who, incidentally, is a collector, and has written a learned article on Bellarmine jugs) writes of a 'blue-dash charger' (an English 'delft' dish) depicting Adam and Eve, that it is:

> A pure ornament,
> An object for one who collects
> Objects, it covers a span
> More than its surface, a truth . . . .

William Empson, in his 'Homage to the British Museum' (1932) writes of a primitive toad-shaped god that used to be in the old Ethnographical Department:

> His smooth wood creeps with all the creeds of the
>   world.
> Attending there let us absorb the cultures of nations
> And dissolve into our judgment all their codes . . . .

Here again is the idea that a particular antique has absorbed something of an earlier time, something which we may be able to distil from it.

In several other poems, antiques are made catalysts for purely personal memories: Thackeray's cane-bottomed chair, Eliza Cook's old arm-chair and old clock, the treasure-box of Robert Graves's 'Ann in Chill Moonlight' or the brass button of Sir Osbert Sitwell's old sahib which

> at a touch
> Fastened two worlds together distant in time and
>   space.

While some of the poets think that antiques help one to recover the past, others see them as poignant relics of a past which can never be restored, reminding us of past ideals superior to those of the present. Robert Bridges says of the crusader on a church brass:

> Would we could teach our sons
> His trust in face of doom.

The late L. P. Hartley, one of the most devoted collectors among modern writers, has a character say in his novel *The Collections* (1972, pp. 14-15):

It seems to me, in these rather sad days, that some people attach more importance, and more affection, to the relics of the past, than they do to their fellow human beings – an object from long ago embodies something we can't recover, because it springs from an impulse which we have outlived, and can only substitute for it images derived from the workings of the mind – laboratory experiments, in fact.

The frailty of antiques is another recurring theme, sometimes as an emblem of human impermanence, sometimes to mock the vanity of setting store by such perishable trifles. The requiems for lost antiques include Coleridge's 'Monody on a Tea-Kettle', George Thornbury's 'Melting the Earl's Plate', and Ella Wheeler Wilcox's 'An Old Fan'. But my favourite is Tom Hood's 'The China Mender', a slapstick classic about a poor man whose engagement is broken off because he breaks his fiancée's mandarins and toads.

But as against those who set too much store by antiques, there are those oblivious to their beauty. On that subject, Samuel Butler's 'Psalm of Montreal', which gave us the immortal catch-phrase 'O God, O Montreal!' is not to be bettered. At the opposite pole – reverence for egregious junk – C. S. Calverley has surely preserved the goofiest collector of all time, the man who saved in a glass case some cherry-stones spat out by the Prince of Wales:

> My cherry stones! I prize them,
> No tongue can tell how much!
> Each lady caller eyes them,
> And madly longs to touch.

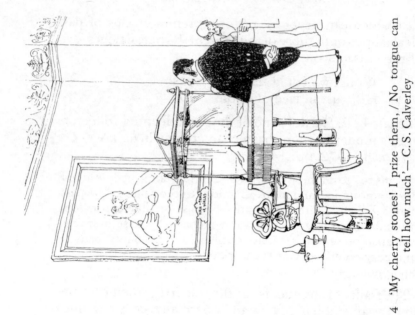

4 'My cherry stones! I prize them, / No tongue can tell how much' — C.S. Calverley

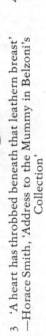

3 'A heart has throbbed beneath that leathern breast' —Horace Smith, 'Address to the Mummy in Belzoni's Collection'

At the same time, poets have been sympathetic to the 'mystique' of antique collecting at its higher levels. Andrew Lang's 'Ballade of Blue China' (1885) claims:

> There's a joy without canker or cark,
> There's a pleasure eternally new,
> 'Tis to gaze on the glaze and the mark
> Of china that's ancient and blue.

These lines more than hint at the escapist character of much collecting. Escapism has always been an element in the collector's cast of mind. Ralph Nevill said of the eccentric nineteenth-century Irish peer Lord Clanricarde that although he was a passionate collector of Sèvres, he took little interest in French history. 'The French Revolution, for instance, did not appeal to him at all; "an unpleasant affair," he told me, "which I don't want to read about." He took very much the same line about the Great War, and when people mentioned it before him would at once change the subject' (*Life and Letters of Lady Dorothy Nevill*, 1919, p. 190).

It was again Lang's 'Palace of Bric-à-Brac' (*Rhymes à la Mode*, 1885) that gave the most elegant expression to this philosophy:

> The foolish people raging
> O'er Bradlaugh and o'er Bright
> They know not the assuaging
> Of what is 'good' and 'right':
> Of coins that 'scaped the Vandals,
> Of daggers with jade handles,
> Of broidered Syrian Sandals,
> Of bowls of malachite.
>
> Can kings or clergies alter
> The crackle on one plate?
> Can creeds or systems palter
> With what is truly great?

We should not be ashamed of the escapism of collecting. As our environment is progressively ruined, there is more and more to escape from. That subject, too, has been eloquently treated in English verse, in the *Letters to Malaya* written in 1947 by Martyn Skinner, who had been an exact contemporary and friend at Magdalen College, Oxford, of the arch-conserver Sir John Betjeman. Skinner wrote:

> Old Regent Street, did war dismantle that?
> War, was it war that laid Adelphi flat,
> Along the river-front on arches borne,
> And from them by some huge explosion torn?
> Or was it a softer sound the terrace shook,
> The sound a cheque makes as it leaves its book?

FURTHER READINGS

Guest, Montague J. (ed.). *Lady Charlotte Schreiber's Journals: Confidences of a Collector of Ceramics and Antiques....* London and New York: John Lane, 1911. *Extracts* edited by the Earl of Bessborough, 2 vols. London: John Murray, 1950, 1952. The life-long reminiscences of the greatest collector of Continental and English porcelain, the bulk of which is now in the Victoria and Albert Museum. She is very candid about stratagems used to obtain bargains and her success in haggling.

Haskell, Francis, and Penny, Nicholas. *Taste and the Antique: The Lure of Classical Sculpture 1500 – 1900.* New Haven and London: Yale University Press, 1981. Traces the rise and decline of interest in antique sculptures. Celebrated by countless poets and novelists, these works were endlessly reproduced in marble, bronze, and lead, and as plaster casts, porcelain figurines for chimney-pieces, and cameos for bracelets and snuffboxes.

Jerningham, Charles Edward, and Bettany, Lewis. *The Bargain Book.* London: Chatto & Windus, 1911. Rambling and genial account of how wonderful it is to collect.

Stillinger, Elizabeth. *The Antiquers: The lives and careers, the deals, the finds, the collections of the men and women who were responsible for the changing taste in American antiques, 1850 – 1930.* New York: Alfred A. Knopf, 1980. A social history explaining the growth of interest in Americana. Those who initially considered American antiques as curiosities in time gave way to collectors who sought to demonstrate that Colonial furnishings could rival European elegance, and eventually to others for whom Americana exemplified an idealized past.

CHAPTER 5

Why Landscapes are Harder to Protect than Buildings

MARION SHOARD

THE COUNTRYSIDE plays an immense role in English national life. There is reason to suppose people care far more about the rural landscape than care about the treasures of the built environment. Three industries – agriculture, forestry and tourism – depend on the countryside. Not that any of these industries employs many people: farmers, farm-workers and those engaged in forestry together make up little more than one per cent of our population; those employed in tourism make up another one per cent. It is the non-industrial activity that thrives in the countryside that plays by far the biggest role in our national life. Visiting the countryside is the second most popular out-door recreation pursuit among British people, beaten only by gardening and ahead of watching and participating in outdoor sports or visiting the seaside, according to a Countryside Commission survey in 1978. There are 300,000 paid-up members of the Royal Society for the Protection of Birds, including 30,000 children and teenagers. Some 20,000 young people make expeditions into wild moor and mountain country in Britain every year in order to qualify for their Duke of Edinburgh's awards. Archaeology and local history, much of it based in the countryside, have in recent years become extremely popular subjects for study in adult education classes, attracting numbers comparable with and sometimes greater than those studying traditional subjects like music, English and politics.

This active involvement in the countryside on the part of so many people is accompanied by real interest in and affection for the countryside on the part of many other people who don't actually visit it themselves. For the English countryside is inextricably bound up with our national identity. The quality of the English countryside has helped shape the English character just as that same countryside has shaped much of England's art. Try and imagine Chaucer, Constable, Shakespeare, Turner or Elgar brought up in a foreign country.

In spite of the deeply-felt concern for landscape, and the relatively narrow base of enthusiasm for buildings, it is buildings which have won the protection of the law while landscape has been left defenceless. Yet it is the country-side that is under threat, not our towns and cities. The landscape is at the mercy of the small group (under one per cent of the population) who own it and farm it for profit. These people are currently intent on making major changes in their methods which threaten to destroy the countryside as it is enjoyed by others. And they are armed with the power to make virtually whatever changes they wish without reference to anybody else – a situation quite unmatched in the built environment.

Britain's town and country planning system is the envy of much of the world. But in spite of its name, it relates effectively only to towns: Britain's countryside is not really subject to government in the public interest at all. All that is controlled in the countryside is urban-type development — in effect, buildings, whether they be houses, electricity pylons, factories, hypermarkets or new towns. Farming and forestry are almost completely exempt from the effects of planning controls. When Attlee's 1947 Town and Country Planning Act nationalized development rights in land, it excluded from its definition of the 'development' for which planning permission would be required before a particular change could go ahead, all farming and forestry activities.

In 1947, the exemption for agriculture from planning control did not appear to carry with it a threat to the landscape. The impact of farming operations on the countryside was much less far-reaching in the years leading up to 1947 than it has been since the early 1960s. Indeed, conservationists of the 1930s and 40s saw farming as a buttress against landscape change: the main threats to the countryside were seen as ribbon housing development, factory building, mineral excavation and unsightly advertisement hoardings.

Now, however, a new agricultural revolution is under way whose impact on the landscape dwarfs that of all other changes to the countryside in the last two hundred years. Advances in agricultural technology and rising subsidies to agriculture have combined to encourage farmers to remove landscape features on uncultivated land in order to grow as much food as possible. Guaranteed minimum prices even for products which are in surplus make it profitable to plough up almost any square inch of ground, and the machinery to make this possible is now available.

Seventy per cent of England's land surface is countryside and few corners of it remain unaffected by this agricultural revolution. No sudden transformation has occurred, but bit by bit England's traditional patchwork quilt of fields downs and woods, separated by tree-studded hedgerows, sunken lanes and sparkling streams has been disappearing. Over large areas, the countryside has taken on a bleak and empty character. Already a quarter of our hedgerows, 24 million hedgerow trees (more than twice the number killed by Dutch elm disease), thousands of acres of heath, down and moor, a third of our small woods, and hundreds upon hundreds of ponds, streams, marshes and flower-rich meadows have been eliminated as the English countryside is gradually turned into a featureless expanse of prairie, its surface given over either to cereal growing or to a grass monoculture fuelling intensive stock-rearing.

In the face of all this, the town and country planning system has been powerless. For what has been happening does not constitute 'development' as defined in the Act. No serious attempt has yet been made by the Government to come to grips with the threat by extending the Act, or by other means. The problem calls for action to rationalize the unequal struggle between competing uses of rural land. What's happened instead is simply that the established rural interest groups have been left to entrench their position. As a result the English people look like being stripped of their rural birthright.

Yet it was to head off a comparable threat to our urban environment that the town planning system was created. The Town and Country Planning Act of 1947 was an attempt to stop the process of urban despoliation which in the 1930s threatened to do to our towns and cities what it did in fact do to many of their American counterparts. The system has the effect of limiting the power of landowners to override other interests by requiring them to seek the consent of the community before they change the environment. A man who wishes to turn his hotel into a factory, his sweet shop into a supermarket or his house into two flats must first apply to his local planning authority to ensure that his plans would not unduly disadvantage other members of the community. If he fails to convince, he must drop his plans. In the countryside, the man who owns the land may uproot hundreds of miles of hedgerows if he wishes, fell trees, drain marshlands, streams and ponds no matter how great their natural history interest. He may plough up hundreds of acres of open moor, heath and down even though other people and their forefathers may have enjoyed access to it for recreation for generations, without any requirement to notify or consult, let alone seek consent from the rest of the community. Even where buildings are concerned, farmers enjoy special privileges. A man needs planning permission before he can put up the smallest house in town or country, or extend an existing house. But a farmer can erect industrial buildings on his land equivalent in area to eight tennis courts and up to forty feet in height without the need for any planning permission at all.

Technically, all land in England belongs to the Crown and the people we speak of as landowners have simply acquired certain rights over it, the most extensive of which are termed freehold. This approach offers an excellent basis for determining land use in a way which will ensure the maximum benefit for most people. But this is not how rights over rural land have come to be viewed in practice. We speak of land*owners* and we attribute to individuals the same rights of ownership of rural land as those we attach, say, to a transistor radio set but not, say, to children or pets, whose owners are not allowed to treat their chattels as they wish. England's countryside may technically have been nationalized by medieval kings, but at the moment it is still in practice in the hands of barons who are not required to take any notice at all of the needs of other members of the community who have an interest in the countryside. In fact some of them have chosen to forego profit in the interest of conservation. But the transform- ation of the English countryside over the last twenty years demonstrates that many more are understandably reluctant to make this sacrifice voluntarily. The attitude of many of them can be summed up in the line attributed to a Suffolk farmer by the *East Anglian Daily Times* of 7 January 1981: 'There is no more place for a hedge in a wheat field than there is for a hedgehog on the factory floor of Ford's Dagenham'.

It is revealing to compare the protection afforded to historic buildings with that afforded to historic landscapes. Two hundred and seventy-five thousand buildings in England have been 'listed' on a central register compiled by the Department of the Environment. All surviving build- ings from before 1700 are automatically listed; others are selected on account of their special architectural or historical importance. It is this listing which has ensured that so many British towns and cities still contain many old buildings. If the owner of a listed building wishes to demolish or alter that building in a way that could affect its special historical or architectural value – for instance, through altering a staircase or a wall – he has to apply to his local planning authority for special permission known as listed building consent, in addition to any planning permission that may be necessary. If either kind of permission is refused, the owner receives no compensation. In addition to tough enforcement powers to conserve listed buildings, local authorities have the right to designate whole districts as Conservation Areas within which special permission is needed for the demolition of all buildings, listed or not.

If half of Britain's historic buildings were now actively being destroyed, there would be a national outcry. But this is what is happening to the relics from the past that lie in the countryside. Causewayed camps and Celtic fields, cliff castles and chambered long barrows, cromlechs and cursi, standing stones and saucer barrows still litter England's countryside and provide the only clues to the nature of life in Britain for the 50,000 years of human existence in these islands before written records were kept. Hedgerows, shaws, country parklands, medieval fishponds, ancient coppices, the remains of ridge and furrow reveal much of what the records fail to tell about life during recorded historical time. Most ancient features in our countryside have never been excavated, but thousands of the archaeological sites that provide the raw data for history are destroyed ever year, mainly by agriculture. Most at risk are relics that lie under marginal land like chalk downland, heather moorland and woodland. Much of this land has lain uncultivated for centuries, entombing evidence for man's activities at times when the land was cultivated or used as a meeting place, a settlement, a site for religious celebration or whatever.

Wiltshire is a county that has seen its landscape transformed since the war, as rough chalk downland turf formerly used for sheep grazing has been turned into a huge barley prairie. Forty per cent of the county's most important archaeological sites were destroyed in the process in just ten years between 1954 and 1964. It is now not merely particular sites that are in danger; whole categories of historic landscape feature are being wiped out. Only 10 per cent of south Dorset's recorded total of 871 Bronze

Age burial mounds had survived undamaged by 1963 and ten years later only 5 per cent were left. Ninety-four per cent of the settlements known as 'rounds', established in Cornwall in the Iron Age and Roman-British times two thousand years ago, were being sliced through with plough-shares in 1979; in the same year 54 per cent of the Neolithic long barrows of the Cotswolds – great stone mausoleums providing virtually the only evidence of the way of life of the Neolithic peoples who came to settle there in 4000 BC – were being destroyed.

What is being lost embraces an enormous range of things. The importance of archaeological and historical features does not end with their documentary value. These features are fundamental to the interest, variety, regional identity and air of magic that distinguishes England's countryside. The special sense of place evoked by Dartmoor, west Cornwall, the Dorset Downs and the Weald, for example, relies heavily on the upstanding relics that freckle the land. For many people, the presence of relics of ancient man enhances a sense of remoteness from contemporary life. The sense of the past that visitors to these landscapes breathe in is reflected in the literature, poetry and painting that has sprung from them. By allowing these features be cleared away, we allow areas of countryside to be robbed of their special character; they become just like any other bit of England of the last quarter of the twentieth century.

Some protection even against agriculture and forestry is afforded to a small fraction of archaeological sites in England's countryside: the Ancient Monuments and Archaeological Areas Act of 1979, expected to come into force during 1981, requires any person who wishes to alter or destroy any of the 8,000 archaeological sites in Britain's countryside that are scheduled ancient monuments to seek consent from the Secretary of State for the Environment. Applicants refused consent for any building development or mineral excavation get no compensation, but farmers are entitled to compensation for profit foregone if consent is refused for an agricultural operation that would damage or destroy a site. Unfortunately, compensating farmers for refraining from activities like ploughing down and moor, grubbing up woods and hedgerows or draining wet meadows is very expensive. As only half a million pounds has been set aside to cover compensation in the first year of operation of the new controls, it is clear that consent for ploughing is not going to be held back very often. To make matters worse, scheduling affects only an estimated one per cent of archaeological sites in Britain's countryside; and historical features like hedgerows (many of which are up to two thousand years old), trackways, old deer parks and the gardens of country houses are explicitly excluded from scheduling.

Thus we protect only a fraction of the historical record that the landscape embodies. What man has built with bricks and mortar and is of some historical and architectural value is usually secure. But the evidence of his past and the beauty and interest of the countryside embodied in ancient hedgerows, shaws, parks, trackways, countless archaeological features and the shape of the landscape itself stands defenceless in the face of an accelerating process of destruction.

Why do we devote much money and energy to protecting buildings but more or less ignore the countryside in which they lie? The answer to this question is manifold. In particular, certain fundamental characteristics of landscape make it much more difficult to administer in the public interest than buildings; some of the most destructive changes in our landscape are difficult to detect, certainly at first glance; and our cultural tradition upholds the right of those who make money from the countryside to determine its destiny. Let's look at these three reasons one by one.

The elusive character of landscape

First, the characteristics of landscape itself. We understand buildings: our fellow men shaped them for purposes we can understand. But landscapes are different. They are the product of interaction between man's works and the geography, geology and biology of our planet. A trained naturalist, archaeologist, farmer, forester or sportsman can interpret landscape to a limited degree. But no-one is expert enough in all the disciplines necessary to grasp all that is involved in one piece of countryside. To most of us, who neither work in the countryside nor specialize in the study of an aspect of it, any landscape is essentially a jumble of objects whose origin, function and relationship to each other are mysteries.

A second characteristic of landscape which poses problems for conservationists is the difficulty of defining the limits to any particular stretch of it in space and time.

The built environment is organized in easily defined units: villages, towns, historic town centres, stretches of 1930s suburbia and so on. The countryside is different. Most landscapes appear like seamless webs that merge into one another quite imperceptibly. A few enclosed tracts of landscape are fairly easy to define in the mind's eye: gardens or country parklands, almost always enclosed by a wall; unenclosed commons in built-up areas or in intensely farmed countryside. But most landscapes appear indeterminate. Even the components that make up a landscape are less clear-cut than those that form the building-blocks of built-up areas. Hedgerows erupt into spinneys and woods; a patchwork of bracken and heather merges into a patchwork of ryegrass and barley; a field becomes progressively wetter as it leads into a marsh or stream. This feature of landscape brings any idea of regulation up against the difficulty of definition of the area and type of area to be covered. But it carries with it another problem too. Because landscape is indeterminate, it appears to many people inexhaustible as well. It seems that even if one tract of landscape has been robbed of its character and interest, then there will surely be another unspoilt tract over the next hill or round the next bend.

In a town we can distinguish at a glance and hence feel

concern about individual houses, factories, roads, town halls and so on. We can also instantly tell the age of a building. Old buildings are selected for listing and therefore conservation on account of their architectural and historical importance. If a Norman church or a Georgian theatre were being demolished, many people would notice and protest, but how many could feel sure enough that the hedgebank or ancient woodland they saw being cleared was of historic interest, to rouse the alarm?

So ignorant are most of us of the age of most of the landscape around us that a complete misconception has taken root. It is now widely but erroneously believed that the traditional English countryside is only about 200 or 500 years old. Letters in *The Times* during the debate about conflicts of interest between modern agriculture and conservation in the autumn of 1980 illustrated well this error. 'The neat patchwork of fields and hedgerows which has come to be accepted as the quintessential English countryside has existed only since the end of the eighteenth century', wrote one correspondent. Another wrote: 'Five hundred years ago, England was covered in forest'. The belief that our landscape is of recent origin serves as a major obstacle to its conservation. It enables those who intend to destroy it to pose as no more than agents of a tide of change that reshapes the landscape, for better or for worse, every now and then. If this were true, it would still be possible to argue that some changes were more desirable than others. But it is not true at all.

The English countryside as we now see it has actually developed over a period of 6,000 years. To be sure, England was once covered in forest, but this was a post-glacial forest which existed not 500 but 6,000 years ago. Since that time, when Neolithic man began making clearings in the ancient forest to grow crops and to graze livestock, the English countryside has continually adjusted to new demands. The landscape we see today – paths, roads and villages, ancient earthworks, hedgerows and walls, land tilled and land left rough – is the product of thousands of years of social and economic change. This steady process of development has thrice been interrupted, however, by advances in farming methods which have imposed far-reaching and dramatic change on the landscape. The first such revolution was the discovery, shortly before the Roman conquest, that one piece of land could be cultivated again and again, particularly if it were allowed to lie fallow, thus making possible the end of shifting cultivation. Those who think that the countryside was created two hundred years ago mistake the considerable impact of the second agricultural revolution on the landscape for the creation of that landscape. This second revolution, the enclosure of the common land and open fields by landowners, which reached a peak between 1750 and 1850, certainly left its mark on the face of central England: landowners, eager to produce more food for the growing industrial population, imposed a geometrical pattern of hedgerows and stone walls on the old open-field landscape of the Midlands. Outside this area, however, the effect of the second agricultural revolution was much more limited. Most of the hedgerows that survive today outside the Midlands were already in existence when the enclosure movement began. Many date from the times when the first settlers enclosed fields from the primeval forest; others have formed parish boundaries since Saxon times. And even in Midland counties many hedgerows and whole landscapes are much older than two hundred years. Half of Oxfordshire's hedgerows pre-date the Georgian and Victorian periods, and 15 per cent of Oxfordshire's hedge-miles mark out fields carved straight out of ancient forest, according to surveys by landscape historian Frank Emery.

It is not only the age of landscape which is mysterious. Their very form is elusive. Landscapes are always changing. One scene never looks quite the same on another occasion. The pattern of line, form, colour, contrast, scale and focal points that makes up any landscape is at the mercy of light and weather to a much greater extent than is the impression left by a building. And the sense of change in landscape is compounded by the rotation of the seasons with the accompanying activities of man, like the trimming of hedgerows or the harvesting of crops.

This feeling of constant change helps mask the effects of deeper, permanent alterations to a landscape. If buildings, like hedgerows, were decapitated every year, we might find it easier to accept their complete demolition; certainly the removal of hedgerows is not seen automatically as an attack on our heritage. Acts of God, like Dutch elm disease, further accustom us to change in the countryside – even damaging change.

The feeling that the landscape is a shifting creature, as well as of uncertain age, means that an enormous degree of change can be thrust upon it before anybody notices, let alone complains. At the moment we are living in the midst of an agricultural revolution whose impact on the landscape far outweighs the two earlier revolutions. But farmers try to soften the impact of what they are doing on the public mind by emphasizing that the countryside has always been changing and that the existing landscape was itself created by change. This is perfectly true. But it remains as possible to destroy a country's landscape heritage as it is to destroy its historic buildings. And there are all the signs that our landscape heritage is now being destroyed, even though the alarm bells are so muffled.

For the rural conservationist, however, it is the third characteristic of landscape that poses the most insidious problem — apparent ability to regenerate itself. The main constituents of landscapes — plants — clearly do have the power to replicate themselves as obviously as buildings lack this quality. This phenomenon imparts the dangerous illusion that landscapes, once savaged, can be relied upon to heal their own wounds. In fact, far from being able to regenerate themselves, landscapes are often impossible to replace, however much devotion is applied to the task. Buildings can be reassembled stone by stone, even though they do not perform this feat themselves. But we cannot reconstruct even one individual tree – let alone the kaleidoscope of lines, forms and colours that makes up a single landscape.

The insidious course of landscape change

The elusiveness of landscape character is matched by the intractability of landscape change. When a Firestone factory is demolished at least it is obvious that this has happened. And it is clear that demolition is necessarily a painful experience for a building. Yet the changes most threatening to the countryside are often imperceptible to the casual observer and may sound, when casually re-counted, harmless or even beneficial.

The intensification of rough grass pasture is a case in point. Ploughing is one of the oldest activities in the countryside: out of context the verb itself conjures up something slow, steady and reassuring. And ploughing plays as vital a role in most kinds of landscape as the sunshine or the rain: the special beauty of the English countryside depends on a combination of uncultivated land and ploughland. Against this background the news that a tract of ancient downland turf is being ploughed up will not arouse the same popular outrage as might the news that it was being buried in concrete or eroded by visitors' feet or cars. Yet building and erosion from recreation affect only a tiny amount of downland compared with the amount being eliminated by ploughing. Since the war, thousands of acres not only of chalk downland turf, but also of all our other main types of rough, flower-spangled, grazing grassland have been sliced up by the plough, sprayed with huge quantities of pesticide and then sown either with barley or with perennial ryegrass, which happens to be convertible to milk more quickly than the old rough grasses on which cows used to feed directly. The process is drawing a blanket of uniformity over a countryside which used to be different-iated partly by the variety of its grazing pasture.

This subtle process of agricultural change has obliter-ated much of the open land on which people used to walk, picnic, ride and play; it has destroyed archaeological treasures that had lain undisturbed under the soil surface for thousands of years; and it has eliminated a wealth of wild creatures. The loss of recreation areas ranges from vast tracts of chalk downland turf in Sussex, Hampshire, Dorset and Wiltshire that thirty years ago provided land over which the walker could roam at will on a carpet of springy, thyme-scented turf, speckled with upstanding archaeological relics and rich in animal and plant life, to small tracts of marshland, perhaps used for tadpoling for generations, that have been drained, reseeded and fenced off. One quarter of Dorset's downland turf, or 11,000 acres, for instance, went under the plough between 1957 and 1972 – downland that harboured nearly 120 different species of flowering plant as well as 20 species of grass. With the flowers go the butterflies. Twenty-four of Britain's butterfly species can live in natural permanent pasture, but not a single British species can live in reseeded ryegrass. The Nature Conservancy Council has estimated that if all farmland in Britain were totally 'improved' we would lose 80 per cent of the birds and 95 per cent of the butterfly species from our farmed lands. But the scale of this threat is far from apparent to the casual observer. After all, the countryside still exists; the grass is still green albeit a different, more vivid shade; and, from the air, our land still looks variegated because different crops continue to be grown on adjacent fields.

Tree planting is another deceptive phenomenon, in one sense more deceptive than roughland ploughing. For tree planting is actually presented as a means of restoring to the landscape some of the character which farmers' operations have destroyed. Plant a few trees behind you and nature will restore everything modern agriculture has taken away, many farmers would have you believe. Several local authorities and official bodies like the Countryside Commission do seem to believe that tree planting is a sufficient means of covering farmers' tracks. The approach of Essex County Council is typical: it consists of giving farmers grants to plant trees and offering them advice on the management of any landscape features they choose to refrain from destroying. The chairman of Essex County Council's Planning committee made his Council's approach clear in a letter published in *The Times* on 13 November 1980:

Hundreds, possibly thousands of small spinneys have been planted over the length and breadth of Essex. But this is only one side of landscape conservation: a typical visit by one of my countryside staff will include advice on the age and management of hedgerows, small woodlands and ponds; the improvement of farm buildings by a coat of bitumen; the farmer's rights (as well as the public's) with regard to footpaths and bridleways.

The Essex countryside today, studded as it is with the fruits of the County Council's excellent tree-planting schemes, does not, however, bear comparison with the landscape shown in photographs of pre-war Essex. No amount of tree-planting can re-create a countryside of flower-spangled downs and marshes, fragrant meadows and thick hedgerows, coastal marshes and sparkling streams, primrose woods, and sunken, violet-studded banks. Nor can it compensate for the disappearance of truly irreplaceable features – the secrets of our nation's past enshrined in archaeological features or Britain's ancient woods, those relics of the post-Ice-Age forest cover that were taken into management through coppicing and pollarding in medieval times and whose plant and animal communities, undisturbed by land clearance, have been undergoing a gradual evolution through thousands of years. Yet in the last thirty years, clearance of these ancient woods to replace them either with farm crops or with fast-growing conifers has destroyed nearly a third of the ancient woods that had survived in Britain from time immemorial until 1945. Nonetheless, palliatives like tree planting can still be presented to innocent audiences as evidence of concern for the landscape, and the confusion is the greater because some tree planting is, and much more could be, a genuine transfusion service for a countryside being steadily drained of life.

The obstructive content of our cultural tradition

The assumption that the countryside can look after itself is reinforced by our cultural tradition. It is traditional to assume that those who own and work the land – the people who are making most of the changes to our landscapes – know best what should be done. Radio and television series like 'The Archers' and 'Emmerdale Farm' convey the familiar idea that the countryside, and in particular the agricultural environment, breeds more wholesome people than do our towns and cities. Professor Gerald Wibberley explains when this classical tradition became particularly popular:

The uncritical belief that human character fashioned by rural, and particularly by agricultural, experience was somehow vital to the development of a healthy nation, was fostered in the rapidly growing industrial climate of nineteenth-century Britain. So much of the literature of the time bewails the passing of rural Arcadia and its replacement by the dark satanic mills and hateful conditions of the industrial city (Joan Davidson and Gerald Wibberley, *Planning and the Rural Environment*, London: Pergamon, 1977).

And with our assumptions about the essential goodness of country-dwellers goes a belief that farmers know better than mere city-dwellers not just how to administer the land but what form it should take. The National Farmers' Union argues that because farmers created the landscape, we have only to ensure the future prosperity of farmers to guarantee ourselves a beautiful landscape in the years ahead. The problem is that the agriculture that helped shape the countryside was completely different in its effect on the landscape from the activity that now goes by the same name.

The approach of the Countryside Commission to country-side conservation and in particular to the conflicts of interest that can arise between modern agriculture and conservation shows how successful the farmers can be at pushing their line. The Commission would not for one moment contemplate the removal of planning controls on industrialists like mineral operators, or those who build houses, factories or offices; but it has always said that there is no need for planning controls over agriculture: instead it advocates a campaign of education and advice to farmers, hoping that this will be sufficient to persuade farmers to go against their own economic interests. The Commission believes that farmers should be free to decide when and where the activities they wish to carry out for economic reasons should be modified or abandoned in the interests of the rest of the community, even though it would not dream of placing the same burden of responsibility on those in charge of other industries. In fact, the Commission's attitude is probably largely governed by the belief that the extension of planning controls to the countryside is impracticable, given the power of the farming lobby in Britain. The only function then remaining for conserv-ationists is to appeal to the better nature of a group whose power is inviolable – an appeal that had best be made in polite terms for fear of enraging those to whom it is made.

Even more distorted than our picture of the men and women who run the countryside is our idea of the nature of their industry. We are constantly bombarded by the media with a completely false picture of the present-day rural scene. We are not shown a countryside ravaged by modern agriculture over large areas in which most animals are kept indoors, farmers and farmworkers are nowhere to be seen and the land itself is a biological desert. Instead, we see a countryside of little cattle-grazed fields, enclosed by neat hedgerows and served by a Dan Archer figure amongst traditional farm buildings, all reassuring us that the present-day rural scene is still as beautiful as it was when we were children. And this reinforces the notion in the minds of many of us that agriculture is not an industrial process at all. From the time when cities first existed, men have returned to the countryside to regain contact with earthy, primitive rural tasks: one of the major tasks of the rural conservationist today is the unappealing but necessary one of pointing out that modern agriculture has wiped out the countryside's nymphs and shepherds.

Agriculture in Britain today is no longer a process that can be summed up in the lines 'We plough the fields and scatter / The good seed on the land / But it is fed and watered / By Gods Almighty hand'. It is, rather, an industrial process involving the conversion of one set of industrial products into another set that happen to be edible. The amount of nitrogen-based fertilizer applied to UK farmland increased eightfold between 1953 and 1976; over a similar period the number of approved pesticides in use on British farmland increased twelvefold. Today there are more than 500,000 tractors at work on British farms, compared with 10,000 in 1920; while the 300,000 horses still working on our farms in 1950 have now virtually all disappeared.

Yet the image of agriculture that is beamed down by a wide range of media is something quite different from the industrial process that agriculture now is. Harlech Television's weekly programme 'West Country Farming', for example, is introduced by a film of two horses slowly drawing a plough through the soil; a similar picture greets the reader on the cover of the *Farm Holiday Guide* for 1979.

In contrast with our beliefs about the innate goodness and worthiness of farmers is the stereotyped but also mistaken view of the urban visitor to the countryside. Farmer Leonard Griffiths, writing in *The Times* on 7 November 1980, deployed this familiar image in his argument that farmers should continue to be given *carte blanche* to change the countryside for their own ends. He wrote: 'Fewer people walk in the countryside today than formerly and it is not because the footpaths are no longer there or because farmers prevent them from doing so. The fact is that they arrive in the countryside in their motor cars but they then refuse to get out of the wretched vehicle to walk – wheels must take them everywhere.' The stereotypical urban visitor to the countryside is a creature unwilling to venture beyond his roadside picnic area, where he reads the *Sunday Mirror* and drinks tea from a flask without even venturing outside his car, save perhaps to toss bulky items of domestic refuse into hedges, trample down orchids and leave farm gates open. If this were the true face of rural recreation it clearly would not matter much what farmers or foresters did to the landscape, but it is not.

The countryside is used by a great many people for a wide range of activities. Professor Colin Buchanan put this point well in a letter to *The Times* on 18 November 1980:

Surely the point about the countryside is that it is used for so many different purposes. Farming is one; looking at it from cars or trains is another. It is also used for exercise, for rambling, for camping, for riding, for adventure-training, and it provides source material for artists, poets, biologists, ornithologists, zoologists, archaeologists, architects, historians and many other people. It also supports other life forms for which, it could be argued, we humans with our unlimited powers of destruction, have special responsibilities beyond the fact that we may find them interesting or beautiful. All these interests, with the possible exception of farming, would seem to be better served by the green field system than by prairies. Is not this the context in which modern agricultural processes need to be judged?

The problem in arguing about conflicting interests in the countryside is that this multiplicity of groups that make use of the countryside can convey no immediate, meaningful image on the public mind. Farmers, in contrast, are seen as a clearly defined group who perform a vital function; few people know a farmer personally, but everybody can immediately recognize the stereotype. Those who seek to question some of the things farmers do can rely on no pre-established image of reassurance, if they can rely on any image at all. When I was interviewed on 'West Country Farming' on 1 February 1981, the description that appeared on the screen of the function I fulfilled was 'environmentalist'. Not the programme's fault, of course, but what image exactly did that designation conjure up?

The food weapon

Those seeking to resist the conservation of landscape have in their hands a propaganda weapon denied to those seeking change in the built environment. On the whole, property speculators building office blocks, industrialists seeking to install processes which create noise and pollution can expect to have to prove that the change they want is desirable. Farmers, however, do not owe their exemption from the need to justify land use changes they want to carefully prepared evidence demonstrating that what they do is in the national interest. They do not have to. Instead they are able to rely on the emotive appeal of one simple idea – 'food'. This slogan is not supported by argument for the very good reason that in today's conditions there is no real argument to support it. This does not matter. The slogan is magical enough to do its work unsupported.

The arguments on which the National Farmers' Union and the Ministry of Agriculture now rely to justify granting farmers continued exemption from planning controls and to justify their massive state subsidy do not stand up to a moment's scrutiny. For instance, the idea that agriculture should be subsidized by the state in order to produce exports runs counter to the present Goverment's and the last Labour Government's economic strategy for all other industries: they receive state subsidy not as an open-ended commitment but in order to tide them over difficult periods if there is a good chance that these industries will be profitable at the end of the day. Even if it were thought wise to subsidize industries to produce exports, there are far more obvious recipients of whatever money might be available for this purpose than agriculture – other industries too that employ far more people than farming. The original idea for supporting agriculture was based on the need for the country to be able to feed itself in time of war, but it is plainly absurd to argue that we need to plough up all our marginal, uncultivated land now in order to be self-sufficient in food, for on our present diet with more than

90 per cent of our farmland producing animal feed rather than crops man can consume directly, we could never be self-sufficient; and in the event of a blockade several experts have shown that we could feed ourselves by switching the mix of crops we grow – a privation we would all presumably be prepared to accept in the circumstances – on an acreage of land smaller than that which is at present under the plough.

The farming lobby seems aware that the case for intensification as a public good (as opposed to a means of enrichment for farmers) does not stand up to close scrutiny. But it is also aware that the mere mention of the food argument can stir deep emotional disquiet. The president of the National Farmers' Union has only to rise up at a meeting and utter a sentence including the word 'food'; however weak the argument on which his case is based, the reassuring image he imparts, the magic in which he will try to enshrine the process of food production and above all the underlying scariness of the idea of starvation, provide him with an extremely powerful platform.

This position is very different from that of the maligned property speculator facing the massed ranks of his well-organized foes at an urban public inquiry, even though the development the speculator proposes may often be of far more benefit to the community in terms of income or employment than everything the farmers have done in the countryside since Attlee's Government enthroned them in their position of unchallenged privilege.

The difficulties of justifying landscape preservation

The protection of old buildings is justified primarily on historical and architectural grounds. Most land-use decision-makers seem at ease with the idea of preserving buildings because they are old, because they represent a particular style of architecture, or because they are of special historical interest. But the reasons for preserving most landscapes are far less easy to describe and to categorise.

The reason usually given for the conservation of land-scapes is 'natural beauty'. All ten of our National Parks and all thirty-three Areas of Outstanding Natural Beauty – the two main types of protective landscape classification in England and Wales – owe their selection and protection largely to this concept, on the assumption that individual people may well have different preferences for different sorts of landscape but that there is nonetheless a consensus view on what constitutes an attractive scene. But land-use decision-makers seem to find it hard to accomodate landscape considerations much of the time. And when land-use decision-makers *do* take landscape considerations into account, they often tend to interpret 'beauty' to mean what suits them, justifying their actions with the old cliché that 'beauty is in the eye of the beholder'.

Apart from the essential vagueness of the idea of 'natural beauty' as the basis for the protection of landscapes, it has two other major disadvantages. First, the expression 'natural beauty', which alone is used to justify the selection and protection of our Areas of Outstanding Natural Beauty, reflects only one aspect of their importance. These are not just aesthetically pleasing landscapes: they also play a vital role in our national life. Our most valuable landscapes – like the Wye Valley, the Hampshire Downs and the Northumberland and Cornwall Coasts AONBs – usually embrace the countryside of greatest recreational importance. Hunting, shooting and fishing, canoeing, orienteering and bird-watching, driving, riding and walking are all enjoyed most intensively in the most attractive parts of the countryside. But though these activities are important to all sections of the community, they are not considered grounds in themselves for the protection of the environments in which they take place.

Secondly, no criterion advanced for conserving land-scapes – scientific, historical, recreational or aesthetic – can be adequately costed and therefore weighed against economic criteria in the way to which planners are accustomed. But natural beauty is at a particular disadvantage in the planner's world of computers and cost-benefit analysis since there is no way in which the beauty of a landscape or the impact of a proposed change on landscape character can usefully even be quantified. All conservation does of course involve some value judgement: although the importance of a listed building is assessed on more specific criteria like age, architectural importance and technological innovation, the listing decision often involves some value judgement – perhaps concerning its importance in the local scene or its attractiveness. The evaluation of a landscape requires much more subjective judgement: there are no objective criteria like age. All we can do is to describe landscapes and ask observers who are as far as possible representative of the community at large to decide that one landscape is more aesthetically pleasing than another.

Wilderness landscapes provide perhaps the most intractable problems of definition. In Britain it is heather and grass moorland that is considered by leading countryside conservationists to fulfil most completely the role of wilderness environment – a place in which people, usually singly or in small groups, can roam at will and feel completely cut off from twentieth-century urban life. But although the protection of large areas as wilderness has even come to dominate some aspects of countryside policy-making, in particular the selection of national parks, the criteria for wilderness preservation have never been translated into a set of guidelines in the way that a mass of analytical advice has been prepared by central government on the selection and preservation of historic buildings. In fact, this lack of explicit criteria has not held back the conservation of wilderness too seriously, as even if criteria have not been articulated, some idea of the qualities of a wilderness as wild, open, assymetrical, homogeneous, high up, open to free wandering and devoid of twentieth-century man's activities can be hypothesized fairly easily. Clearly the enclosure of moorland country for intensive farming or afforestation by conifers clashes with unspoken requirements. It is the more subtle idea of the indubitably man-made lowland farmed landscape which throws up the greatest problems in justifying landscape conservation. Unfortunately it is this landscape which modern agricultural methods most threaten to wipe out.

There is, however, one feature of landscape protection that matches exactly a common problem in the conservation of buildings. The protection of landscapes that are scientifically, historically or in some other way unique or at least scarce is much easier to achieve than that of landscapes that are simply important for people in their day-to-day lives. Building conservationists will recognize the problem. Dotted all over England's countryside are thousands of odd pieces of uncultivated, marginal land supporting hedgerows, spinneys, woods, rough meadows, marshes and streams which may not be of any special wildlife or archaeological note but which play an important role in people's lives. People in towns and villages all over our country may use such land for an early morning stroll or jog or to exercise their dogs. Their children go there after school to climb trees, to catch tadpoles and play chase. These tracts of marginal land stand to be 'reclaimed' at any time by farmers and in fact such pieces of land are now disappearing at an alarming rate.

Landscape features, particularly those which lie near our homes, form part of our collective identity. We are, in part, the places that have shaped our lives. If England's landscape is impoverished, so are our personalities. In their chapter, Tamara Hareven and Randolph Langenbach argue for the protection of buildings which are important in people's lives whether or not the buildings in question happen to be of special historic or architectural note. 'The principal reason why we seek to preserve our heritage is to preserve our own identity, to give us a point of reference from which we can measure ourselves', said Patrick A. Faulkner, the Superintending Architect of the Ancient Monuments and Historic Buildings Division of the Department of the Environment (*Journal of the Royal Society of Arts*,

Vol. 126 (1978), p. 458). This should be as true of landscapes as it is of buildings.

In conclusion, it will always be more difficult to protect landscapes than to protect buildings. But we can no longer use this difficulty as an excuse for leaving the task unattempted. The time has come when we must find out how what has been achieved in the conservation of historic buildings can be achieved in the more intractable realm of landscape. For it now seems that our landscape needs protection more than our historic buildings have ever done.

FURTHER READING

Berry, Wendell. *The Unsettling of America. Culture and Agriculture.* San Francisco: Sierra Club; New York: Avon Books, 1977. Examines the impact of modern agriculture on the American landscape and calls for the replacement of large farming units with small-scale, mixed family farms.

Millman, Roger, and Brandon, Peter F. (eds). *Historic Landscapes: Identification, Recording and Management* (1978); *Recording Historic Landscapes* (1980); *The Threat to the Historic Rural Landscape* (1981). Department of Geography, Polytechnic of North London, Occasional Papers. Three conference reports summing up the state of historic landscape conservation in Britain.

Newby, Howard. *Green and Pleasant Land? Social Change in Rural England.* London: Hutchinson, 1979; Harmondsworth: Penguin, 1980. Examines the impact of the post-war agricultural revolution on the social fabric of the English countryside.

Sheail, John. *Rural Conservation in Inter-War Britain.* Oxford: Clarendon Press; New York: Oxford University Press, 1981. Describes the conditions and thinking that gave rise to Britain's town and country planning system.

Shoard, Marion. *The Theft of the Countryside.* London: Maurice Temple Smith, 1980. Examines the nature of the current agricultural revolution, its impact on the English countryside, the adequacy of landscape defence machinery to meet this threat, and economic justifications for agricultural change. To conserve the countryside against agricultural change, I recommend the extension of planning control to the farmed countryside, the establishment of new regional countryside authorities, the designation of six new national parks in lowland England, and the improvement of access to the countryside, particularly for city dwellers.

Turner, Keith. *The Impact of Modern Farming Systems on the Social and Physical Environment.* The Mill House, Olney, Bucks: Nuffield Farming Scholarships Trust, 1980. Compares the impact of agricultural change on the countryside in Britain with that in France, Romania, Denmark and West Germany.

CHAPTER 6

Living Places, Work Places and Historical Identity

TAMARA K. HAREVEN and RANDOLPH LANGENBACH

> The action of time makes man's works into natural objects... In making them natural objects also time gives to man's life-less productions the brief quality of everything belonging to nature – life.
>
> *Vernon Lee*, 'In Praise of Old Houses' (1902)

IN 1975, a member of the wrecking crew working on the demolition of the massive, once famous, but now faded housing project in Leeds, Quarry Hill Flats, noticed among the people watching that one couple had tears in their eyes. Turning to them he asked, 'How can you cry over something like this?' Their response was, 'We had lots of good times here' (a story related by Alison Ravetz, July 1978). Historians and conservationists in Britain have ignored the demise of Quarry Hill Flats. The housing project was generally unloved by the larger community and unwanted by the city. It was quite simply not old enough to be considered a preservation issue. But some of the people who had lived there experienced a deep sense of loss when the structures with which they had identified a major part of their lives were ruthlessly and unceremoniously swept out from beneath them.

Similarly, in New England, former residents of Boston's West End who had been uprooted from their communities returned annually to the empty lots where their houses once stood. The blessing of the home, a ceremony which they carried out once a year, brought them back from the suburban housing project where urban renewal had relocated them to what they considered their real home.

The West End residents' attachment was not just to an individual home. Most of them had lived there in tenement flats. Their identification with their individual residences was reinforced by the kinship and friendship networks which permeated entire streets. Their attachment to the physical structures drew its strength from their identification with the texture of the entire neighbourhood, an identification inseparable from the physical setting.

What invests buildings with life? How do they emerge into the consciousness of people as entities possessing an intangible worth beyond their usefulness or the value of their brick and stone? Is there a basic difference between what they mean to the 'informed' architectural expert or conservationist, and what they mean to the people whose lives are interwoven with them?

The environment of historic industrial cities and towns in the United States and Great Britain provides an unusual setting for examining the social issues involved in the conservation of the built environment. Many of these cities have recently been experiencing economic and physical change at a rate never before encountered since their origins.

These urban industrial environments also stand at another point of transition: the symbolic meaning which the nineteenth-century industrial building conveys is changing, and buildings and sites suddenly are regarded as 'antique' instead of simply 'old'. We are currently living at a unique historical moment, with remarkable but highly transient opportunities to reflect on the meaning of the historic work and living places within these communities before they either disappear or become subject to formal preservation efforts. Memories of the active use of these buildings during their prime are fading, but still accessible for a limited time in a generation now dying out.

Shifting American attitudes towards the remains of the nation's industrial heritage are most dramatically marked

5 Amoskeag Mills, Manchester, New Hampshire

by the transformation of deteriorated and neglected industrial Lowell, Massachusetts, into a new National Park, just a decade after the demolition of the mills in Lowell's sister city, Manchester, N.H., under a government-financed urban renewal project. Ironically, Manchester's complex of mills and workers' housing had been better preserved than had any complex in Lowell. Lowell, the oldest of the planned industrial cities in New England, is certainly worthy of preservation. The fact that Lowell was declared a National Park shortly after the massive demolition of the mills and company housing in Manchester underscores the reversal.

Britain's industrial heritage is experiencing a somewhat different fate. The preservation of surviving artifacts from the early period of the Industrial Revolution has attracted widespread interest and support. However, much of the industrial landscape and cityscape in Britain, as in the United States, dates from the late nineteenth century. To many people this industrial landscape seems too recent and too ubiquitous to warrant being preserved.

The change in attitude described for the United States is, however, also becoming more evident in Britain. Interest based on personal associations, such as that expressed by the couple at Quarry Hill, is converging with concerns based on history and architecture and with general commitment to these industrial landscapes as essential elements in the nation's identity. The surviving physical environment of nineteenth-century Pennine industrial towns today adds the personal memories of everyday life, which has since changed dramatically, to an abstract and generalized textbook knowledge of history. A woman from a mill town in Cheshire wrote in response to the SAVE-sponsored 'Satanic Mills' exhibition shown at the Royal Institute of British Architects in 1979:

I thought I was the only person in the world who loved old mills. We could see 25 or so factory chimneys from the school window. One mill was particularly beautiful...equal (in my opinion) to the Chateaux of the Loire, complete with tower and

6   Quarry Hill Flats, Leeds, demolished 1977

7   Huddersfield mills being eroded by demolition

wrought-iron ornamentation... I used to pass the weaving shed on the Stack Mills on the way to school. The flagstones were hot and vibrating. Children would take their mothers chips, black peas, steak and kidney puddings in at dinner time. There was a crèche at Ashton Bros. a long time ago to cater for women who worked the machinery... my mother-in-law started work in the paper mill at 11 years old – 6 o'clock start, bread and dripping for breakfast at 8, soup at 12, bread at 4, finish at 6. And no talking allowed.

The personal experience has become part of the folk-lore of the community. That in turn is now beginning to be transformed and legitimized into history – a history which is slowly being accepted as important by a larger society. The letter reveals the significance of memories of everyday life – a way of life people struggled through but accepted despite its overwhelming difficulties, but which has since been swept away, except for the *buildings* which survive as silent witnesses. These buildings provide the continuity elicited in this recall. The hope this woman expressed that the mill with the tower 'is still there' should not be misconstrued as a wish to return to the old days of the work at eleven years of age and the breakfast of bread and dripping. Rather, it is a wish that the memory of life she had known should not be unhinged from reality through the destruction of the principal elements of its setting. People's identification with buildings is partly shaped by earlier stages in their life-cycle which the building symbolizes. Ernest Anderson, a former mill worker in the Amoskeag Mills, then seventy-five years old, related for our book *Amoskeag* (1978, p. 147): 'Sometimes I take a walk through the millyard. A lot of it is torn down today; but as I look up, I can see those mills, how they flourished at one time, and I don't feel as old as I am.'

We are saddened by the sight of an individual suffering amnesia. But we are often less concerned or aware when an entire community is subjected to what amounts to social amnesia as a result of massive clearance or alteration of the physical setting. The demolition of dwellings and factory buildings wipes out a significant chapter of the history of a place. Even if it does not erase them from local memory it tends to reduce or eliminate the recall of that memory, rendering less meaningful the communication of that heritage to a new generation. Such destruction deprives people of tangible manifestations of their identity.

The more locally restricted is such identification, the greater the deprivation. Demolition of an industrial working or living environment most severely affects the working class, especially its elderly members. Contrary to the commonly-held belief that it is these groups which have the most to gain by replacement of old or outmoded houses and workplaces, they are the most likely to suffer displacement as a result of demolition. A West Yorkshireman quoted in Marie Hartley and Joan Ingilby, *Life and Transition in West Yorkshire* (1976, p. 91), expressed the impact which slum clearance had on him. 'When t'old square went summot else went wi' it that all t' posh tahn centres in t'world can't fetch back.'

The condemnation and clearance of physical structures can be read as a condemnation of the way of life which had been lived there. In his *Loss and Change* (1974, p. 55), Peter Marris pinpoints the issue most poignantly:

They would like more space, better drains, repairs – but to achieve this only at the cost of destroying the neighbourhood itself seems to them an inconceivable distortion of what is important. If the physical setting has one meaning to the planning authority, it has another to the residents. The corner shops, the shabby streets, the yards and lots... are invested with all kinds of intimate associations. They identify with the neighbourhood: it is part of them, and to hear it condemned as a slum is a condemnation of themselves too.

Beyond their links with individual identity, buildings perform an important role in the historical memory of a community. While abandoned mills may signal the decline of an industry, the same buildings, no matter what their current condition, may also symbolize past power and success.

Planners, politicians, and urban reformers often assume that people hate the buildings they once worked in because of their association with poor working conditions and exploitation. But those who make such claims about workers' feelings have seldom actually worked in such buildings themselves. It is the mistaken impression of middle-class civic leaders (many of whom are from regions other than the city in question) that since conditions were worse then than they are now, people must wish to forget the past and would prefer to see its manifestations erased.

The assumptions of social reformers and planners that the working-class past in these industrial settings must be eradicated because it symbolizes poverty, grimness, and exploitation, misses what the workers themselves feel about their world. Most of the former industrial workers whom we interviewed for the Amoskeag oral history project remembered the good and the bad as inseparable parts of their life's experience. They were willing, and at times eager, to recall the bitter times along with the good. Both were part of their entire life story and were deeply enmeshed with their sense of place. Memories of struggle with poverty, daily two-mile walks to the factory, unemployment and strikes, illness and death were all part of that story, and were intimately linked to the buildings. Beyond their individual experiences, buildings were so significant to people's memories because of their associations with other people, such as family members, friends, neighbours, and fellow workers, with whom they had shared these experiences.

While the outside world of reformers and planners condemned the buildings and the experiences of textile work which they represented, the people who actually worked in those buildings saw them as inseparable parts of their lives. Those whom we found to hold negative attitudes had advanced into the middle class, and felt that association with these buildings conflicted with their efforts to escape from their parents' working-class

116

background. As is often the case, however, the grand-children of those who had worked in the mills have sometimes turned to appreciate and value the world of their grandparents, while the intervening generation rejects them. In this instance, the middle generation, which is currently at the centre of community power and influence, has deprived the older as well as the younger generation of the continuity in the presence of structures which conveyed an important association with the city's identification.

Our argument about the significant role which buildings play in the formation of identity is not contingent on the assumption that people spend their entire lives in the same neighbourhood. Both American and British society have experienced extensive geographic mobility over the last two hundred years. Indeed, the question needs to be asked: if people are so mobile why does historic preser-vation make such a difference?

The attachment of people to individual buildings or to entire neighbourhoods is both real and symbolic. In Boston's West End, London's East End, or Leeds's Quarry Hill, the physical attachment of people to the neighbourhood was intertwined with kinship and neighbourhood and institutional ties, and destruction of the neighbourhood also fragmented the social community.

People become attached to certain buildings because of the association with past or present experience, which the buildings symbolize, even if that experience has not been a continuous part of their lives. An attachment formed initially with a certain building can be transferred to other buildings of the same type in other places. Thus, people who had identified with certain buildings in their residences or work-places in one community would seek out similar types of buildings in another community. Whether or not they formed new attachments they would still live with the special memory of the original buildings and relate to them when the opportunity arose.

Identification with a building is not restricted to people

living in its immediate environs. Its destruction can remove a symbol meaningful to people living there who happen to know it from past experience. What counts is the symbolic value of the building – the way of life and the sense of continuity which it represents. People identify with a genre of buildings not only because of their environmental quality but also because of the particular role they had filled. The survival of buildings and landmarks associated with a familiar way of life provides continuity of social as well as physical fibre. The more mobile a society, the greater the value of the continuity symbolized by these buildings.

Recently, Americans have begun to counteract feelings of rootlessness by embarking on the reconstruction of individual family genealogies and collective oral histories of communities. Buildings and familiar landscapes play a significant part in this need and search for identity. As Marris says in *Loss and Change* (p. 150):

Conservationists are often ridiculed for wanting to keep old buildings or familiar landmarks which are neither beautiful nor historically important. But the townscape ought to reflect our need for continuity, and the more rapidly society changes, the less readily should we abandon anything familiar which can still be made to serve a purpose. Even if a sweeping redesign would be more efficient, more practical, more beautiful, even if those who used it would come to prefer it, I think we should still consider whether such abrupt discontinuities are worth the stresses they set up. There is a virtue in rehabilitating familiar forms which neither economic logic nor conventional criteria of taste can fully take into account, and we should at least recognise this, before we decide what to destroy.

The past is not a constant. Every generation reinterprets its own history. Perceptions of the past and myths upheld by different generations have a significance that transcends whatever one might seek to define as 'objective historical reality'.

The artifacts of different periods thus gain in status and historical significance as attitudes change towards their historical period and style. In the United States, Victorian antiques have begun to take a respectable place next to early American, and in the 1980s Art Deco and Depression Era artifacts are coming into their own. This progressive recognition and acceptance of objects from more recent periods is not merely the result of the passing of time; it is also connected with the coming of age of generations whose tastes are less elitist and more accepting of the industrial heritage.

The increasing recognition of vernacular, especially industrial, buildings as a legitimate part of the historical heritage is part of this process. The growing historic consciousness of the value of the work-place represents a recent departure from an elitist approach not only to buildings but to the industrial heritage in general. It parallels the rediscovery of social and labour history as the heritage of the common people.

Buildings derive absolute historical importance not alone from their creation in a particular period, or from their established aesthetic and stylistic value, but also from the social context in which they were used, the functions they fulfilled, and the historical experiences associated with them. This is precisely why the rediscovery of vernacular buildings is part of the rediscovery of a new past – a past which encompasses the lives of common people.

Historical consciousness has recently expanded in two directions. First, the scope of historical scholarship and interest has broadened to include groups which had previously been neglected, such as industrial workers, village labourers, slaves, immigrants, and migrants. Second, social historical endeavours have encompassed social experiences which were not previously recognized as legitimate aspects of historical scholarship, such as work and leisure, childhood, old age, and family life. This shift in historical consciousness has led not only from elites to common people, but from official, public history to a history of private lives and experiences; in short, from formal and institutional to a more existential history.

119

With these changes, the criteria for the historical values of buildings change too: buildings are 'historical' not only because they are associated with the lives of elites, or because they are public monuments. Buildings become important because of their association with the private work and family lives of large numbers of common people in the past.

This development is not entirely new. There has been for some time an interest in the dwellings, work-places, and artifacts of everyday life from the remote past. Medieval or Tudor villages, colonial or nineteenth-century American settlements, antebellum slave cottages, all have been elevated to historical status and turned into museums, because they tell the story of everyday life in the past. The problem is how to accord such status to buildings which do not represent remote eras, but times within the experience of people alive today or their parents and grandparents. The significant task is not only to recognize the historical value of working and living areas, but also to acknowledge buildings from the more recent past as legitimately historical.

The recovery of the life histories of common people in the past, as part of a larger effort to reconstruct a whole society and to make anonymous voices heard, has not been fully matched by the recognition of their places of residence and work as legitimate historical structures. There is currently a gap between the legitimation of the social and cultural history of common people, and the acceptance of vernacular structures as historical monuments. Entire living and working environments of unusual historic and architectural quality are still being destroyed. For example, at the Sett Mill in Oldham, a remarkable surviving example of a small early-nineteenth-century mill village with two owners' houses, two facing rows of workers' houses and the mill, the houses have been unceremoniously removed as 'unfit' by the Borough. The settlement was all the more remarkable because the two brothers who owned it lived in houses attached to the ends of the rows of their workers' houses. Until quite recently one was still occupied by the 80-year-old Mrs Sett, who, along with the residents of the workers' houses (some of whom were former employees of the Sett Mill), was evicted from her own house.

Official recognition of outstanding sites, such as the transformation of the remnants of the Lowell mills into a National Park, and the establishment of the Quarry Bank Mill Museum in Styal as a historical monument, are moves in a positive direction. But to establish genuine links between community identity and the built environment, we need to preserve not only the exceptional, symbolic specimen, but local work-places and neighbourhoods. Ironically, artificial mill museums, using artifacts stripped from genuinely historic and intact mill villages, have been established in the United States in particular.

The challenge of conservation is to preserve the meaning of the way of life which buildings represent to those who have worked and lived in them, as well as the more abstract and formal qualities based on knowledge of architectural and technological history. Many times one has passed a registered national landmark with its bronze plaque and formal parking area, visited by parties of school-children and by tourists from abroad. The visitors to these monuments become informed by their visit, but rarely are they genuinely moved. Often what they find is a monument so sterilized as to be devoid of any real impression of its use over time – sterilized of the 'life' identified by Vernon Lee above. At Covent Garden, for example, the extent and quality of restoration has, to a degree, removed the visible effects of its use as a market. This wear and patina of age is what one associates with an historical market and it can be disorientating to find it so entirely removed when the market is turned into an uncharacteristically elegant shopping centre. This problem is more apparent in the United States, where reconstructions such as Colonial Williamsburg in Virginia often blur the line between real and fabricated history, distorting the context in which what is genuine can be appreciated and understood.

The problem for planners and preservationists dealing with such a timely and evocative subject as the nineteenth-century industrial landscape is how to weld together in the preservation effort the two aspects of human association, the intimate, and that based on knowledge of art and history. Historical and architectural scholarship can give credibility to personal feelings and a sense of identification, while individual associations can give vitality to the historical interpretation. An example is the Gladstone Pottery Museum in Stoke-on-Trent, which has integrated the presentation of folklore with preservation of obsolete industrial structures. The pottery craft continued in the museum buildings and the periodic ceremonial firing of surviving bottle kilns in the area, bring out surviving workers from the days of the handfired kilns, and stimulate an exchange of knowledge and feeling, injecting vitality into the museum project.

Some critics who condemn conservation as elitist question whether working-class housing occupants and factory employees have an aesthetic response to buildings, implying that if they do not, there is little point in preserving them. We have found some people in all walks of life who do respond aesthetically and others who do not, but the virtues of conservation do not depend on an aesthetic response. This is not to deny the value of the scholar's definition of worth, based on comparative historical or architectural criteria. But conservation broadly considered must juxtapose general criteria of social history and architectural analysis with the meaning that buildings have for local rehabilitation in terms of personal experiences.

Preservation is in a sense a *community* act. It is as important as a process as in its results, contributing to the mutual education of people who see beauty and value in terms of architecture or of a building's place in the history of engineering, technology, or town planning, and those who know simply that the buildings and places are meaningful in terms of their own lives. Successful conservation can rarely result from the actions of either group alone. It is most effective when it reflects a coming together of people from both backgrounds. As a conservation effort becomes a real force in a community, the diversity of its roots within the community and the multiplicity of its goals for different people proves to be its most stimulating aspect. Conservation provides a chance to draw these diverse parts of a community together, using the physical fabric of the past as a matrix for people to achieve a greater understanding of each other.

FURTHER READING

Brolin, Brent C. *The Failure of Modern Architecture*. Cincinnati: Van Nostrand Reinhold, 1976. Modern architecture discussed in relation to history, style, social conditions and user perception.

Hareven, Tamara K., and Langenbach, Randolph. *Amoskeag: Life and Work in an American Factory City*. New York: Pantheon Books, 1978. An oral history of former factory workers in Manchester, New Hampshire, which illustrates from the interviewees' own perceptions their strong identification with the physical setting of architectural environment.

Huxtable, Ada Louise. *Will They Ever Finish Bruckner Boulevard?* New York: Macmillan, 1963; London: Collier-Macmillan, 1972. A collection of Huxtable's *New York Times* architecture columns, sharply drawing the battle lines of specific preservation/redevelopment issues.

Marris, Peter. *Loss and Change*. London: Routledge & Kegan Paul; New York: Pantheon, 1974. A theoretical study of the sense of loss which accompanies personal and social change. People are stated to have a 'conservative impulse', a need to maintain continuity.

Ravetz, Alison. *Model Estate, Planned Housing at Quarry Hill, Leeds*. London: Croom Helm, 1974. A brilliant analysis of the abbreviated life of Quarry Hill flats and an account of their destruction.

Thompson, Michael. *Rubbish Theory: The Creation and Destruction of Value*. Oxford and New York: Oxford University Press, 1979. An incisive assessment of how things, including buildings, lose and gain value as they age. This book adds greatly to an understanding of the historical significance of conservation.

Tuan, Yi-Fu. *Topophilia: A Study of Environmental Perception, Attitudes, and Values*. Englewood Cliffs, New Jersey: Prentice-Hall, 1974.

Part III

LOCALITY, COMMUNITY AND CONSERVATION

THE PAST involves us at all scales of experience – individual, local, regional, national, global. Most of the essays in this book deal with preservation issues on a universal or national level, or in terms of purely personal responses. But action as well as attitude is usually strongly influenced, if not determined, by local groups. Viewed from a town, a suburb, a neighbourhood, or a rural area, preservation priorities seem quite different than when seen from Whitehall or Washington. The structure and history of the local community, the quality of development, the extent of residential participation in decision-making all affect approaches toward what has survived or is deemed worthy of preservation.

The case studies in Part III explore how people in four diverse English localities deal with the historic landscapes and structures they live with and wish to save. Leeds and Suffolk, Metroland and Dartmoor each exhibits its own combination of antiquities, treasured because they are singular or familiar, grand or commonplace. These four chapters also demonstrate that intimate knowledge of a place is needed to achieve a proper conservation rationale, let alone any lasting success.

Sylvia Sayer recounts the history of efforts to save Dartmoor's landscape and Iron-Age antiquities from farming, from military degradation, and from industrial pressure. Local preservationists have long joined forces with outsiders attracted by Dartmoor's elemental majesty. Today, those who seek to preserve this awesome moorland must also cope with the erosive effects of tourist popularity.

They have the advantage of the Dartmoor Preservation Association's unified and vigorous leadership.

To preserve and adapt to modern needs Suffolk's wealth of historic features – farmhouses, town dwellings, churches, watermills, and, not least, landscape elements of which more than half have been lost since the Second World War – is the daunting task of many scattered local organizations. As urban overspill and retirement settlement transform the county, local amenity groups benefit increasingly from the expertise and pragmatism of the Suffolk Preservaion Society. John Popham shows how the Society's efforts are bent not simply toward keeping what is precious from the past, but toward a viable combination of old with new structures in both town and countryside.

In inner Leeds, development forces that have been destroying the physical fabric and the social community are resisted by increasingly articulate neighbourhood communities. Ken Powell shows how local groups have organized to stem the erosion of housing and other amenities that often occurs in the wake of 'slum clearance'. The loss of local retail outlets to large shopping centres and the threats that social restructuring poses to community landmarks, notably churches and schools, often leave neighbourhoods bereft of all but a few sad and seedy pubs.

Inhabitants of North London suburbs anxious to keep links with the past concentrate on conservation issues of a different character. Matthew Saunders shows how some seek to preserve rural and pre-suburban landmarks, while others focus on Edwardian and later structures. Revival architecture and period evocations of thatching and half-timbering reflect Metroland's nostalgia as much as do its few surviving original relics.

The preservation community in each of these four areas is as distinctive as the landscape, yet they manifest important features in common. Although otherwise utterly different, Dartmoor and inner Leeds both elicit from at least some local residents the concerted devotion to familiar scenes that can come only from a self-aware locality. Neither

Suffolk nor Metroland are cohesive communities in this sense, but rather aggregations with amorphous boundaries and dispersed residential loyalties. Such areas, which lack the compelling force of true localities, often rely on umbrella organizations to co-ordinate preservation.

The case studies also illumine crucial distinctions between urban and rural preservation. In both Leeds and outer London local residents have struggled to save their heritage and familiar neighbourhoods largely without help, except for such exceptional landmarks as Leeds's Quarry Hill Flats and London's Alexandra Palace – the first gone, the second threatened. In the countryside, external support is integral to preservation. Local roots and hereditary zeal fuel the Dartmoor Preservation Association, but without a wider network of moorland enthusiasts local preservationists would have found it much harder to keep the china-clay industry at bay, let alone agriculture and the army. County-based families dominate Suffolk preservation groups, but an increasing proportion of their members, energy, and expertise comes from newcomers, many of them still London-based.

These English locales are microcosms of preservation patterns elsewhere. Changing patterns of residence, especially growing urbanization, tend to shift the emphasis from local community solidarity to the maintenance of physical fabric. Four basic types of locality emerge, two urban and two rural, exhibiting different balances of effort by insiders and outsiders.

One type is the relatively small number of cities and towns whose historic features are so widely valued that national, even international, support helps to ensure their essential preservation. Venice and Nuremburg are obvious examples, but several great capital cities – Rome, London, Paris – also benefit from being everyone's heritage. But the most substantial beneficiaries, both of preservation expertise and of tourist receipts, are smaller and more purely historical places like Carcassonne, Bath and York. Here the historical fabric seems more likely to be secure, though such places do risk degeneration into tourist showplaces devoid of social integrity.

For the vast majority of urban areas, outsiders' interest in their heritage is almost nil. As in Leeds, local residents must carry the sole burden of saving what they deem important. Limited in funds and in political leverage, local preservationists have to balance conflicting demands. On the one hand, pride in local identity compels them to save features of architectural merit and civic significance; on the other, neighbourhood preservation focuses on scenes precious because congenial and familiar. Moreover, pressures for economic and social redevelopment continually affect the choice of what to save and what to let go. Hence the surviving past in such places is always in flux.

Rural scenes exhibit similar distinctions. Relatively few locales have scenic qualities that endear them to large numbers of outsiders. In famous landscapes like Dartmoor or the Lake District the built environment plays a minor role, and preservation concentrates on saving the landscape itself from exploitation and disfiguring artifacts. In rural localities widely appreciated for the harmony of their built and natural elements, like Cotswold villages, Devon hamlets and New England towns, efforts focus on saving and refurbishing the building stock and ensuring that repairs and new structures are in keeping with the old. But gentrification preserves the physical fabric at the cost of the social, whose decline is hastened by the inflated prices fetched by converted old cottages. Often all that is left is a stage-set in a landscape divorced from the community.

Most other rural areas, however, are increasingly neglected by both locals and outsiders. Not found scenic by tourists, they are progressively abandoned by residents; social and physical fabric decline in concert. Depopulation leaves landscapes littered with abandoned dwellings whose ruins bespeak the death of present and past alike. Yet it is just such areas that subsequently serve to rekindle interest in the past. For abandonment and natural erosion, however painfully evident, are apt to be slower and less sweeping than are deliberate demolition, technological improvement, or ill-judged rehabilitation in better-favoured locales.

CHAPTER 7

Wild Landscape: Dartmoor – the Influence and Inspiration of its Past

SYLVIA SAYER

PROBABLY FEW people would deny that wild country or 'wilderness land' is now, in overpopulated Britain, a scarce resource, and that it is being eroded at an accelerating rate – as Exmoor's recent history painfully demonstrates. Dartmoor's once great expanse of moorland is shrinking too, as grant-aided fencing followed by so-called agricultural improvement, commercial afforestation and mineral mining progressively eat up the rocks and the heather, destroying many of the prehistoric and historic remains that are essentially part of the character of the moor.

Certainly there has been a National Parks Act and a Countryside Act and a Sandford Report and a Porchester Report and another Wild Life and Countryside bill, subject to fierce controversy, but whatever the torrent of printed and spoken words what is lacking is not so much in the legislation as in the legislators. The real determination, dedication and will to save wild country appears to be present in only a relatively few Members of Parliament, and even fewer Ministers for the Environment have yet demonstrated an active recognition of the value of our last wildernesses (though Michael Heseltine gives us grounds for hope). The BBC commentator, Gerald Priestland, said of the late President Johnson that he would be remembered for his efforts, with his wife's, to conserve America's natural beauty. No prime minister of ours has yet earned a similar tribute. It is quite hard to believe that any ever will.

And this in spite of many warnings from accepted experts in the environmental field. Sir Frank Fraser

Darling's Reith lectures on 'Wilderness and Plenty' created a stir in 1969 when he was courageous enough to say that we do not even need to justify the survival of wild country in terms of human recreation or landscape appreciation. 'The wilderness', he said, 'does not exist *for* our re-creation or delectation. This is something we gain from its great function of *being*, with the oceans part of the guardianship of the world in which we have come so recently to be a denizen' (p. 85). We are light-years away from getting that particular truth through to the consciousness of those who govern us.

Men who climb mountains seem able to see the situation in particularly clear perspective; theirs, not surprisingly is the long view. Sir Edmund Hillary says in his autobiography *Nothing Venture, Nothing Win* (1977) that 'There are plenty of tamed wonders for all to goggle at through vehicle windows – we must retain our wilderness areas where nature can develop its own calm way and where those humans who are prepared to walk and sweat a little are prepared to go'; and another mountaineer, Chris Brasher, has stated his belief that 'a nation that expands until it has intruded into all its wild land is a nation that has lost its soul. Once the wilderness has gone, there is little escape from materialism' ('Cry the Beloved Wilderness,' *Observer*, 9 February 1975).

The late Anthony Crosland sometimes accused conservationists of being a middle-class elite, but the truth is that far from being a pampered elite the solitary walkers and wilderness-seekers are the underdogs in our community. It is the motorist who is the privileged citizen in the Dartmoor National Park today. Disproportionately large sums of public money are spent on road widenings, car parks, lay-bys and loos, all of which attract more and more motorists into the National Park, although for most of the year Dartmoor is gasping under its tourist burden. The minority of the population that longs for, and needs, the space and solitude of wild country is literally being crowded out; so too are the adventurous young who need some risk and challenge in their lives.

131

Many other wilderness-destroying elements are also hard at work. Among the worst are the activities of the Ministry of Defence, resulting not only in damage to the terrain (an average of 50 shellholes to the acre in one ironically designated Site of Special Scientific Interest) and the destruction of ancient monuments, but also in the construction of a network of military roads in the wildest areas of the moor. Another threat is a 1979 Department of Energy intention to promote the drilling of a number of test boreholes to find out whether this National Park can become a 'dry hot rock energy source', with consequences that can all too easily be foreseen. Conversion of open moorland to cultivable farmland and the threat posed to ancient monuments by ploughing is a perennial problem. Far from being a highly protected area, Dartmoor is in fact a kind of Naboth's Vineyard, in which every type of predatory exploiter competes to stake a claim.

It may be thought that I am straying from the title of my theme, but it is necessary to explain why some of us fight so hard to halt this progressive degradation, earning for ourselves the name of 'extremist' in the process. It is hardly surprising that Dartmoor is a battleground, that its fate and its future arouse fierce passions and cause memorable contests, for the threatened minority will not submit with meekness to the slow destruction of what they regard as a vital element in the quality of life to be safeguarded not only for themselves but for their own and others' children and grandchildren.

So there are dogged defensive actions, backs to the wall, adrenalin constantly flowing, time and money sacrificed, relations grieved, acquaintances lost; but it is all enormously worthwhile; all the time there is the deep satisfaction of knowing that this is a battle not solely to save a last wilderness and the living past but also against greed and materialism. Few causes could be more inspiring.

Dartmoor possesses a peculiar magic and potency, and there seem to be no half-measures about people's feelings for it – either it captivates or it repels. Some visitors cannot

8 Dartmoor: Bronze Age hut circle on Shaugh Moor, saved in 1977
   from obliteration under a vast china clay waste tip

9 Dartmoor: military vehicle damage to area surrounding the menhir
   on Langstone Moor

bear to be alone in its silent spaces; with others the attraction is immediate, as it was with Kenneth Day, who in his book *The Dartmoor Scene* (1946) attested: 'It is now many years since I first visited Dartmoor but from that time onward I have been completely under its spell. There are parts of the country that undoubtedly provide grander scenery, but it is doubtful whether any other region has so great an individuality and so strong a personality.' 'Personality' is an unusual word to use in describing a particular region, but it is certainly appropriate to Dartmoor.

Dartmoor's strong attraction in part derives from the wordless influence of the numerous prehistoric and medieval sites with which it is so richly endowed. Whether or not you are interested in archaeology or history, you can never entirely ignore the presence of Dartmoor's past. The greatest of all Dartmoor authorities, William Crossing, who knew Dartmoor as no one else ever has or perhaps ever will, said truly in his 1912 *Guide*:

To enable the visitor to learn what Dartmoor really is...he should be led from the beaten track to wander among the hills...where silence broods over the sea of fen and the pasture grounds of the cattle that range at will are as they were when the Norman herdsman drove his beasts there...It is here that he comes truly under the spell of the moor; henceforth he can never think of its solitary valleys without looking down through the ages.

As you approach Dartmoor's heights from the cultivated Devon lowlands the centuries fall away faster than the mileage until finally you arrive in the landscape of the Bronze Age; and sometimes this brings a kind of involuntary recognition that you have been here before – a long time before – and that here are your roots, this is your tribal land. And I cannot believe that anyone could be quite unmoved by the experience of standing within the ruined walls of a certain medieval Dartmoor longhouse, aware that its thirteenth-century inhabitants had had to flee from a fire that caused its turf roof to fall in and bury not only their cooking pots and platters but also, in the haste of their retreat, a silver penny of Henry III! It was a labour of love to clear the ruin of the gorse and brambles that at one time hid it from sight.

I am lucky enough to live in an ancient longhouse myself, made more comfortable, it is true, since the time of Henry III, but still essentially a longhouse of the traditional Dartmoor type, built in a valley inhabited from prehistoric times. It is thrilling to dig up in the garden worked flint implements four thousand years old, pottery fragments from the Saxon occupation and iron half-shoes made to fit the cloven hoofs of the little working oxen that were once stalled in what is now our living room.

The astonishing archaeological endowment of Dartmoor is not yet fully known or recorded. Within the past few years a wide area of southern Dartmoor has been re-surveyed by Mr Norman Quinnell of the Ordnance Survey's Archaeological Branch, who has identified twice as many prehistoric sites as are at present shown on the Ordnance maps. Provided the Government does not indulge in its threatened cheeseparing folly of disbanding the OS Archaeological Branch, northern Dartmoor will be investigated to the same high standard and similar discoveries are certain to be made. It is doubtful whether any other comparable area of land in Europe possesses such a magnificent concentration of surviving prehistoric sites; it is equally doubtful whether many other countries in the world would treat this unique heritage with so little care, or allow it to be subjected to such ceaseless agricultural and industrial destruction and military battering.

Nor, regrettably, are archaeologists themselves entirely blameless. Some of today's professionals who excavate Dartmoor's hut circles and field systems seem to dig with enormous ferocity, totally disembowelling an ancient monument to find out if another lies beneath it, leaving at last a scarified area of tumbled stones and rebuilt replicas, a sight that fills me with rage and sorrow. When in 1977 the Dartmoor Preservation Association prevented a china clay company from burying a complex of Bronze Age sites on

Shaugh Moor under millions of tons of clay waste, we found the Department of the Environment's flying archaeological squad as great a menace as the clay company itself; the archaeological commandos only put away their spades when threatened with legal action for digging up common land, and retreated muttering that they'd be back in thirty years' time.

But these smash-and-grab techniques are, it seems, mercifully becoming outmoded. Air photography can teach us more than the spade. Peter Fowler in his book *Approaches to Archaeology* (1977, pp. 54, 190) says: 'Excavation need no longer be the main source of information for the archaeologist... and in parts of the world it has already been superseded. The main source of information is in the landscape, and is extractable by means other than excavation... Archaeology must develop the maturity and strength to say "no" to excavation'; and this seems also to be the view of Professor Charles Thomas, as incisively expressed in his 1976 De Cardi Lecture, 'After Rescue – What Next?'

When a love of wild country is combined with a hereditary love of the past, the Dartmoor influence has a double potency. For centuries before they came to Dartmoor my mother's forebears farmed on Bodmin Moor, so they may be said to have granite in their blood and to have grown up in the company of the prehistoric stone circles, menhirs and medieval crosses that the two moorlands share, as they shared one geological formation 200 million years ago. My great-grandfather had discovered Dartmoor by the 1850s and eventually settled at Huccaby House on the West Dart river in central Dartmoor. It was the family house for over seventy years; much of my childhood was spent there and it was a place of magical happiness to me.

Getting to one's Dartmoor home in a motorless world was a real achievement and made the joy of being there all the more keenly felt. The children of today who are transported in cars like crated chickens along congested roads to some still more congested and publicized 'beauty spot' for an afternoon amongst the parked cars and ice cream vans have no means of knowing that sense of achievement, of having earned their share of Dartmoor – and they have been robbed, although they do not know it and their parents would not believe it.

My grandfather Robert Burnard's Dartmoor diaries record that in his day you could still see crossbills, ring ouzels, landrails and kingfishers in the West Dart valley; the rivers were full of trout and salmon, the turf of the river banks was untrampled, there were still glowworms in the hedges and wild daffodils growing by the roadsides. The Huccaby ménage lived in and with the Moor; in winter the house was warmed by peat fires and in summer its river meadows yielded good crops of hay.

To say that my grandfather loved Dartmoor would be the understatement of all time. To him it was always 'the grand old moor', and he walked it, photographed it, wrote books about it, gave lectures on it, and with his great friend and kindred spirit Sabine Baring-Gould he investigated and recorded with meticulous care many of its ancient monuments for the reports of a learned society known as the Devonshire Association for the Advancement of Science, Literature and Art.

In all Dartmoor matters I feel as my grandfather felt, and sometimes I seem to be speaking for him and he seems to be speaking through me. So I can understand what Prince Charles meant when he described to Huw Wheldon, who was interviewing him in the television documentary 'Royal Heritage', how intensely he shared his great-great-great-grandmother Queen Victoria's love for the Scottish highlands and how often he recognized his own throughts and feelings in the entries in her Balmoral journals.

Most of Dartmoor belongs to Prince Charles, being part of his Duchy of Cornwall estates, but he has never been given an opportunity to know it; on his rare visits he always seems to be transported at speed across it in a car or in an Army helicopter with a general sitting beside him telling him how indispensable it is as a military training area. Had

Queen Victoria taken her highland holidays at Huccaby instead of at Balmoral, her great-great-great-grandson's inherited interest in wild country might now be providing a more effective protection than anything the Dartmoor Preservation Association is able to achieve!

Not that the DPA has not achieved a great deal in nearly a century of strenuous existence. The Association was founded in 1883 because even then it had become obvious that Dartmoor urgently needed defending; its common land was still being unlawfully enclosed, its ancient monuments were being robbed to provide stone for gateposts and enclosure walls, its rivers were becoming silted by tin and china clay washings, the military were enlarging their artillery ranges on the northern moor and the prison authorities were enclosing a further acreage of moorland.

In its earliest years the Association was a select society of gentlemen of standing and authority who met in Plymouth's Athenaeum and started their deliberations with a glass of sherry. Probably the word 'elite' might fairly have been applied to them then. But for all that, they were dedicated people with a down-to-earth knowledge of the moor, and they used their brains and influence to striking effect, winning a number of legal actions which checked unlawful enclosure and the destruction of prehistoric sites as nothing on Dartmoor had ever done before.

This made 'preservation' a dirty word with many of the locals, as sadly it still often is. In his *Westcountry Sketch Book* (1928) the Dartmoor writer Eden Phillpotts recounts a local farmer's complaint about being prevented by antiquarians from using the stones of a prehistoric circle:

'Why for shouldn't us use these here brave bits and save our sweat and our time? Ban't our time, as be money and food, more to us than the time of these zanies, what haven't got nothing better to do than bleat about stones? Not a 'roundy poundy' must be touched, and not one of they old rows, or walls or nothing. And all our own mind you! They 'old men' picked the best stones for their needs and none troubled them, for 'twas a long time ago afore this here blasted protection society got fussing on the Moor.'...My attitude, unlike the labourer's, was one of obligation to those who had arrested the destruction of the old stones. For they are very good to see and think upon; this granite that vanished hands dragged hopefully to build a home, or sadly to mark a grave, may well be suffered to stand; so may we cherish these old stones, so harmonious, so solemn and so still, that link us yet with the vanished ones, who played their part in the morning of days.

Fifty years later few Dartmoor land workers seek to use these old stones. But their attitude is still essentially that of Eden Phillpotts's 'aged priest of earth'; if they're in the way, get rid of them! and damn the interfering preservationists!

So the Dartmoor Preservation Association has to be a fighting organization; may it always be so. Its membership of about 1,300 is wider and more of a mixture now than in the early days; no pre-meeting sherry now, but a cup of tea and a biscuit while discussions go on. Some of its members are retired people, but most have jobs and can only come to Saturday meetings. It is largely (though not entirely) a middle-class membership. A farming member suggested that the Association should try to recruit more working-class people, 'not people who read the posh newspapers but the ones who read the *Daily Mirror*, because there are more of them'. But a massive local membership is likely to mean the entry of elements that favour unrestricted motoring and caravanning and resent restraints on building or advertising in the National Park. Many local councillors and native Dartmoor inhabitants whose forebears had to fight the moor to wring a living from it are likely to support anything that tames the wilderness, such as more roads, quarries or reservoirs or any other development promising further employment or economic advantage. Dartmoor is unique and of national importance, and can no more be left in the care of local farmers than Oxford's colleges can be left in the care of the car workers of Cowley.

Before the 1940s the attitude of most Devonian town-dwellers towards Dartmoor was more protective and enlightened than it is now. There was heated opposition to the military seizure of the moor; there were protest meetings in civic halls; headlines in the local press featured colourful verses praising Dartmoor's threatened beauty without risk of cynical comment. Now the Devonian attitude is in general harder and more philistine; the military occupation is welcomed by many for the money it brings in; local government is apathetic towards the destruction of beauty, and the national park concept is often seen as a challenge to personal liberty.

Dartmoor's defenders try to work in close co-operation with the National Park Planning Authority. Sometimes things go well, sometimes they do not. They consider us extreme, we consider them to be too permissive to the motorist and expansionist farmer and too hooked on transatlantic-type projects of the 'interpretative' variety. If Dartmoor were not so enduring she would be nearly interpreted to death with information literature, guided walks, tourist trails and beckoning publicity. Over-popularity and over-publicity are already her bane. In the last few years some of the more easily reached monuments such as Grimspound have become as bare and trampled as hen runs. Beaten tracks now lead up to all the more accessible tors and other interesting natural features, with further tracks linking one well-known prehistoric site with another. Dartmoor begins to echo Jacquetta Hawkes's comment in *A Land* (1951, p. 133) on present-day Stonehenge: 'Man made Stonehenge, man has destroyed it.' It has lost its mystery, magic and meaning.

If the population goes on growing what chance is there really of saving the wilderness? The sheer pressure on space and resources may sooner or later over-ride the conservationists' defences and if successive Governments continue to regard natural beauty and freedom of access as expendables, we shall gradually but inevitably find that we have lost them forever.

Optimism revives as one thinks of the younger generation whose hearts are already captured by wild country and who are ready to fight to save it. The silicon-chip era is likely to bring more leisure than can be assimilated without social disorder. Recreational facilities of many kinds will have to be provided to meet the needs of the gregarious, but there is another need that no government will be able to ignore without disaster, and that is the deeply-rooted need to find space and solitude in wild country and to feel the influence and inspiration of its past.

FURTHER READING

Abrahams, Harold (ed.). *Britain's National Parks.* London: Country Life, 1959. With Bell, below, essential reading for those who wish to understand the varied character of our national parks.

Bell, Mervyn (ed.). *Britain's National Parks.* Newton Abbot: David & Charles, 1975.

Burnard, Robert. *Plundered Dartmoor.* Plymouth: 1895. An eye-opener on the earliest threats to Dartmoor's character and beauty.

Crossing, William. *Amid Devonia's Alps* (1888). Reprint, Brian Le Messurier (ed.). Newton Abbot: David & Charles, 1974. Adventurous expeditions on wildest Dartmoor in Victorian times.

Crossing's Guide to Dartmoor (1912). Reprinted, Brian Le Messurier (ed.). Newton Abbot: David & Charles, London: Macdonald, 1965; New York: Taplinger, 1966. No more knowledgeable or comprehensive guide to Dartmoor could ever be produced.

Darling, Frank Fraser. *Wilderness and Plenty.* The Reith Lectures, 1969. London: BBC, 1970. For wilderness-lovers, the greatest of all Reith lectures in book form.

Day, Kenneth F. *Dartmoor Scene: A Series of Camera Studies between Two Bridges and Postbridge.* London: Frederick Muller, 1946. Splendid photographs and descriptions of Devon's last wilderness.

Day, Kenneth F. *Eden Phillpotts on Dartmoor.* Newton Abbot: David & Charles, 1981.

Dickinson, Bickford. *Sabine Baring-Gould, Squarson, Writer and Folklorist, 1834-1924.* Newton Abbot: David & Charles, 1970. This biography by his nephew explains the great man's passionate love for Dartmoor.

Fowler, Peter J. *Approaches to Archaeology.* London: Adam and Charles Black, 1977. The right approaches, too – informed investigation rather than wholesale execution.

Gill, Crispin (ed.). *Dartmoor: A New Study.* Newton Abbot: David & Charles, 1970. Many Dartmoor subjects re-examined by ten well-informed contributors.

Hawkes, Jacquetta. *A Land*. London: Cresset Press, 1951; Newton Abbot: David & Charles, 1978. A brilliant conception of the making of Britain.
Hawkes, Jacquetta. *Man on Earth*. London: Cresset Press, 1954. How, against the background of geological change, man's emergence gave the earth 'a mind of its own'.
Hillary, Edmund. *Nothing Venture, Nothing Win*. Sevenoaks, Kent: Coronet 1977. An inspiring autobiography interpreting the value of wilderness to teeming humanity.
Linehan, Catherine D. 'Deserted Sites and Rabbit Warrens on Dartmoor, Devon', *Medieval Archaeology*, Vol. 10 (1966), pp. 113-44. Reprinted in booklet form. The first detailed description of a deserted medieval settlement on a Dartmoor hillside above Okehampton.
Phillpotts, Eden. *A Westcountry Sketch Book*. London: Hutchinson, 1928. This great Westcountry writer's knowledge of Dartmoor is unique and unsurpassed.
Sayer, Sylvia. *The Outline of Dartmoor's Story*. Ashburton, Devon: Bradford, 1951. History and development of the Moor, with line drawings by the author.
Sayer, Sylvia. *Wild Country: National Asset or Barren Waste?* London: Council for the Protection of Rural England, Standing Committee on National Parks, 1972. In the context of mounting threats to Dartmoor, shows how much the preservation of this rugged moorland with its antiquities means to the nation and to the future.
Thomas, Charles. *After Rescue – What Next?* The Beatrice de Cardi Lecture. London: Council for British Archaeology, 1976.
Worth, R. G. Hansford. *Dartmoor*. Plymouth: compiled from the author's published works and edited by G. M. Spooner and F. Russell, 1953. All this expert's knowledge of Dartmoor's archaeology, history, geology and climate.

CHAPTER 8

Leeds: 'Obsolescence' and the Destruction of the Inner City

KEN POWELL

An aesthetic appreciation of Leeds is of little value, because Leeds has no use for aesthetics.

John Betjeman, 'Leeds: a City of Contrasts' (1937)

THE INNER city, despite the major about-turn in Britain's planning policy which took place in the 1970s, is still under threat. We seem to have quit that planners' dream world in which the whole country would be rebuilt, everybody given a new house and every town and city in the land totally recast. But the inner areas of our great cities demonstrate graphically that demolition and redevelopment, once seen as the forerunners of a better life, can go hand in hand with physical squalor and multiple deprivation. Looking at the worst inner areas of Manchester, Liverpool, Glasgow or Leeds, we might doubt whether the rot can now be stopped. Will the various forms of 'inner city action' produce anything more than new industrial estates and landscaped canal banks? Can the inner city become a decent place to live? Can we recreate that elusive sense of community which we seem to have lost amidst the dust of demolition?

The idea of obsolescence, the notion that the physical fabric of urban Britain needs – if only we could afford it – almost total renewal, is still pervasive. The conservation movement and the impact of economic recession have severely slowed the rebuilding of city centres – much of the centre of Leeds is now an Outstanding Conservation Area. Yet elsewhere destruction goes ahead on a large scale and in a cynical fashion which often makes nonsense of the idea of participation in planning.

143

The motives for clearance are complex. The altruistic desire to improve the environment in which people live is undeniably strong. But the theory of obsolescence – that people need new buildings for a better life – is obviously false. It has been used to support a restructuring of cities founded on the motor-car and on rebuilt city centres, increasingly unhealthy and artificial places cut off from the suburbs where the majority of the population live.

Leeds is a city which lacks the worst horrors of post-war urban Britain and has a good deal to its credit in recent planning. In 1945 Leeds was 'a large dirty town... mostly built of sooty brick', as the Bradfordian J. B. Priestley described it in *English Journey* (1934, p. 186). The city centre was almost wholly Victorian, surrounded by a ring of factories and workshops and by solid ranks of red-brick back-to-backs which to this day comprise one of the most potent and distinctive images of the 'real' Leeds. The worst slums of Victorian Leeds had existed on the fringes of the city, in areas such as Quarry Hill, Kirkgate, the Leylands, and around the river, and forty years ago many of these still survived. There were cellar dwellings to be found in some of the old village centres like Bramley and Hunslet, old cloth-making settlements caught up in the growth of the city.

Victorian Leeds had a mixed economic base. By the mid-nineteenth century it had ceased to be a woollen manu-facturing town of any substance, but engineering and the ready-made clothing trade were to become major employers. The city was always an important market and commercial and administrative centre. Even by 1801 it had outstripped in size every other town in the woollen belt of the West Riding. South Leeds became an area of heavy industry and working-class housing. Middle-class suburbs grew up to the north of the river Aire, in Headingley, Chapel Allerton and Roundhay. The city was clearly divided on class lines.

The first attempts at housing clearance came in the slum areas fringing the centre soon after 1870. Privately-built flats were erected around Marsh Lane, east of the centre and near the parish church, in 1901, and a Corporation scheme in this area followed within a few years. From small beginnings, slum clearance became a massive tide by the 1930s, when the overcrowded but basically attractive Quarry Hill area was cleared. Here was built an heroic scheme designed by the then City Architect, R. A. H. Livett, and inspired by Vienna's Karl Marx Hof. The complete demolition of this huge group of nearly 1,000 flats in recent years was a tragic end to this visionary project – yet the Marsh Lane tenements still stand.

One of the chief promoters of the Quarry Hill scheme and of large-scale clearance elsewhere in the city was Canon Charles Jenkinson, vicar of Holbeck in south Leeds and chairman of the housing committee. Jenkinson was responsible for the demolition of much of his own parish, including the fine Gilbert Scott church of St John. A new church rose amongst the winding crescents of the housing estate at Belle Isle, to which the Holbeck people were moved. This is typical of much of Leeds's inter-war public housing, decent, deriving some inspiration from the Garden City movement but architecturally so pared down as to be dull and characterless.

Social amenities, apart from churches and the odd pub, were singularly absent from the new estates. Back-to-backs were still being built during the 1930s, a fact deplored by Livett, Jenkinson and other 'progressives'. Yet the post-1880 back-to-backs which survive today provide decent and popular housing, while the interwar housing estates are in a state of physical and social decay.

So much for the historical background. Leeds in 1981 has some grounds for self-congratulation. It is a major shopping centre – the chief retail centre in Yorkshire and Humberside – and has been successful in attracting office development. Some of the investment has been directed towards environmental improvement. Yet the city's industrial base has rotted. Between 1951 and 1973, 37,000 manufacturing jobs were lost, while 32,000 jobs were

10   Leeds: housing clearance in Hunslet

11   Leeds: the impact of urban motorways. Since the inner ring road
was built after 1960, almost all the old housing shown has gone

12   Leeds: the isolation of surviving monuments—St Saviour, Ellerby Road

13   Leeds: the traditional corner shop, Rawson Terrace; now demolished

created in the service sector: the City Council alone now employs almost twice as many people as it did in the late 1940s. The local authority's policy is to increase retailing and office space in the centre, and in fifteen years (1961–76) over a million square feet of shopping space was added there. The danger is that Leeds will become a city with a prosperous but uninhabited city centre and a peripheral population cut off from the centre by a ring of derelict inner suburbs given over to prefabricated factory and warehouse units.

These inner suburbs – Woodhouse, Burley, Kirkstall, Armley, Sheepscar, Burmantofts, Harehills, Cross Green, Holbeck and Hunslet – developed around ancient cores as working-class communities in Victorian Leeds. At that time, they were vital, living places, despite the relative poverty of their inhabitants. Richard Hoggart's *The Uses of Literacy* (1957, p. 60) spoke of the sense of territoriality felt by the inhabitants of Hunslet: 'They know it as a group of tribal areas. Pitt Street is certainly one of ours; just as certainly as Prince Consort Street next to it is not. In my own part of Leeds I knew at ten years old, as did all my contemporaries, both the relative status of all the streets around us and where one part shaded into another.' Old Hunslet is still spoken of with affection and pride by older residents. It had an identity which, in the 1930s, extended into speech patterns. You could tell a Hunslet man from 'Wood 'us' man by the way he spoke.

Some housing clearance began in Hunslet in the inter-war years. Yet in 1934 a survey of people in St Jude's parish revealed that, despite the offer of new houses elsewhere, 494 of 685 householders wished to remain in the area. Half of them were content to stay in their existing houses. All these houses were, however, demolished and most of the remainder of Hunslet has gone since the war. In the 1960s the landscape was more radically transformed by the motorways. The huge post-war estates at Seacroft and Whinmoor, on the north-east of the city, have absorbed many Hunslet people. Seacroft was promoted as a 'township' with its own 'town centre', in reality a depressing and unprofitable shopping centre.

Some families have been rehoused in Hunslet itself. Hunslet Grange is a huge and grim complex of deck-access flats, much praised by architectural journals when it was built over a decade ago. The dark concrete buildings, surrounded by threadbare grass, have generated a multitude of problems and the development is intensely unpopular. Most of the residents want to be rehoused elsewhere and there have been calls for the buildings to be demolished. Low-rise housing is now being built in the area on long-cleared sites. It is of mediocre design, taking no account of the better remaining buildings, which include some splendid Victorian pubs.

The pubs are about all that do survive from the past. They are all well-patronized, not least by former residents of the district who return to drink there. Nearly all the churches and chapels have gone. The notable Georgian houses which survived into the 1930s, some of the finest in the Leeds area and evidence of Hunslet's identity as a rural retreat for Leeds merchants in the eighteenth century, have disappeared too. Within the last decade virtually all the shops have suffered the same fate. Ten years ago Waterloo Road, near Hunslet parish church, was a real shopping street, a true centre. Now it is flattened, replaced by a 'district centre' which has the standard supermarket, betting shop, etc. Oddly, nobody seems to have thought of this orgy of destruction as a 'conservation issue'.

The destruction of communities in Leeds is still going on. Leeds plans to demolish five hundred 'sub-standard' houses a year over the next seven years. From the time a house is included in a clearance programme, it takes up to eight years to clear – years of uncertainty and blight during which the area steadily decays, houses become unsaleable and are sold to the Council (and left empty and boarded up), and businesses close. The area dies.

Alison Ravetz has shown how unrealistic definitions of land value enshrined in development plans have driven working-class housing out of the inner city ('Changing Attitudes: the Idea of Value in the Inner City', *Built Environment*, 1978). In areas like Hunslet, land acquired at low cost from householders under compulsory purchase orders has been used to develop factories and warehouses (conveniently serviced by the new roads). The CPOs embody an extension of the well-intentioned housing policies of the past to basically sound housing stock, which has proved flexible and popular enough to merit retention and improvement.

'Community' is hard to define, yet the proven desire of most people to remain in their own area has led to growing resistance to housing clearance, a movement co-ordinated by the Community Housing Party. A 1976 Working Party report, *Gradual Renewal in Leeds*, warns that 'the highly abstract physical standards which define fitness in individual houses must not be used as a blanket excuse for destroying whole communities'. The battle over Leeds housing continues. In 1978 the Leeds Civic Trust, a well-established civic society once loath to become involved in housing issues, gave its support to a group of Armley residents threatened with clearance. The future of the city, argued the Trust, depended on the survival of inner-city housing and coherent communities.

The marvellous character of the surviving townscape of Leeds demands to be recognized and conserved for its inherent quality. It is a city of vistas, of hills and valleys, and the traditional terraced housing takes account of the geography of the place. Ancient common lands, for example, form the 'moors' of Woodhouse, Hunslet and Holbeck, while the old centre of Kirkstall is clustered near the ancient bridge site on the Aire. Real centres grew up in these places, often around churches on old sites.

These centres are now being destroyed in favour of new purpose-built 'district centres' with a supermarket rather than a church at their core. Road-building is still a major cause of destruction. The motorways have been put into cold storage, yet road-widening and other 'improvements' destroy shops, pubs and houses and create yet more unusable land in a city which is full of derelict space (830 acres in inner Leeds). The attractive Holbeck Moor was carved up a few years ago for the M621, with dozens of fine trees felled.

Churches, a crucial element in the townscape, have suffered badly. Housing clearances have made many redundant; the Church of England has implemented a programme for the gradual closure of most of its inner-city churches, with little serious opposition. But the parishioners of two east Leeds churches fought a diocesan scheme to close their churches – and won. The congregations are now increasing, one vicarage now houses a nursery and more housing is to be built in the neighbourhood. Yet St Mary's, Quarry Hill, a fine Regency Gothic church which should have formed the key element in a sensitive redevelopment scheme, was demolished a year ago. Holbeck, which has an attractive, 'villagey' centre, had a fine group formed of the 1830s church of St Matthew, set in a large, leafy graveyard, and a pretty Tudor Gothic school. The school has been demolished, the church is closed and in poor condition. It too faces demolition, unless a use is quickly found. Holbeck will thus have lost the central element in its identity within the city.

The old board schools were another monumental element in the Leeds townscape. Of hard red-brick, often in a version of Gothic, they had a certain grimness yet were well-built and displayed great individuality. New uses might have been sought, assuming that they could no longer meet educational needs, but the great majority have gone. One marvellous survivor is at Woodhouse, where its clock tower is a prominent landmark. New churches and schools in the city (with some notable exceptions) eschew architectural statements in favour of a narrow utilitarianism.

The inner-city, basically working-class areas of Leeds are the *essential* Leeds. Not so phenomenal a Victorian city as Manchester, nor so consistently handsome as neighbouring Bradford (a city built of stone), Leeds derives much of its character from the interaction of buildings and landscape. In some districts great flights of stone steps rose steeply to give access to hillside terraces. Now cheap concrete replaces granite setts and cast-iron bollards and railings.

Victorian housing, though built within strict cost limits by speculative builders, was able to adapt to the terrain. To take one example, Leeds was once rich in fine corners, where buildings extended to occupy the whole of the site. Standardized modern buildings are often surrounded by tiny pieces of waste ground. The housing schemes now being built by private developers within the inner-city arc are of dismal quality, devoid of either urban or the better suburban values.

The inner suburbs are losing their identity, however, not simply because of physical erosion but because their historical role is shrinking. Headingley, where housing ranges from spectacular manufacturers' mansions to back-to-backs, still functions well because it provides for students and for the growing number of professional and middle-class people who want to live within easy reach of the city. Misguided planning policies have indelibly marked Holbeck and Woodhouse as 'undesirable' areas. The threat of clearance and the 'lifeing' of houses (streets are given a fixed life, say of twenty years) remove investment from the area. The steady, piecemeal investment characterized by Jane Jacobs in *The Death and Life of Great American Cities* (1961) as 'gradual money' is removed and the neighbourhood does actually deteriorate.

In such instances, local-authority policies amount to a self-fulfilling prophecy. Empty factories rot because nobody is willing to invest in them – yet the city is short of accommodation for small businesses. Houses empty and are allowed to decay – yet Leeds has a housing waiting list.

Shops also close. In Hunslet four hundred shops were demolished in the late 1960s and early 1970s: just thirty new shops were built. There has been a clear official policy concentrating retail activity in the city centre, in effect in the hands of multiple stores. More than one thousand retailers have gone out of business in Leeds during the last twenty years, while large new shopping precincts have been built in the central area. The consumer is the loser, for choice and competition are reduced, and the visual monotony of the chain stores advances. Without shops, the inner-city fringe will become yet more devitalized and specialist trades may be driven out of Leeds entirely.

One shopping street in the northern fringe of the central area for a time survived the wholesale demolition of surrounding houses in the 1960s by developing as the centre of the local antiques trade. It was a very convenient place for dealers (good access and easy to find) and for potential customers, who could easily visit a number of shops in succession. But the Council applied compulsory purchase orders to the whole street and now everything, except for a few pubs, has been demolished. The antiques trade has gone out to the suburbs; no one has benefited from the clearance. Dewsbury Road, a main route out of Leeds, had until the late 1960s more than a mile of continuous shops. All have gone, replaced by new roads and much 'landscaping'. Yet there is plenty of housing, mostly high-rise, in the area. The residents can now shop only at the Hunslet District Centre, a dreary place with little choice, unless they go by bus to the city centre. And bus fares have nearly trebled in five years.

'The crucial lesson for British planners', wrote R. E. Pahl in *Whose City?* (1970, p. 207), 'is to learn their limitations, and to make these limitations more widely known.' A rescue operation is in progress in the inner-city areas of Britain. The new focus on the inner city is rooted in a recognition that the 'clean sweep' policies of the past have failed. Yet wholesale renewal continues. Conservation has had some notable successes in Leeds, yet it is kept tightly within bounds, hedged in by Department of the Environment lists and Conservation Area boundaries.

In the inner city, clearance and the threat of clearance blight both buildings and lives. Gradual renewal has been accepted as the best course for some areas but elsewhere the local authority blunders ahead with demolition. The prejudice against the back-to-back house is still responsible for the destruction of much sound property. In Chapeltown, the city's main immigrant area, large multi-occupied villas are being pulled down, despite the efforts of some people to renovate them as family homes. Planning policies rationalize existing social and economic trends, polarizing the city centre and the outer suburbs. Broad, conservation-based planning would view the city as an organism in which the health of the whole depends on that of the individual parts.

A radical new approach ought to take as its basis the retention and continued use of all sound buildings and the environmental improvement of the inner city. It would aim at retaining or where necessary recreating neighbourhood character, as has been done at Chapel Allerton, a middle-class suburb where old cottages demolished in the 1960s were replaced by new housing of character. Surviving shopping centres need to be strengthened: they are an asset to the city. Supermarkets, if needed, should be slotted into established groups of shops. In a city composed mostly of council housing and chain stores, people will become increasingly apathetic about their surroundings. The open layout of some recent estates is very unpopular with tenants. Their large grassed areas, poorly maintained by the Council, are seen as a no-man's-land, which it is no one's business to keep tidy; they soon deteriorate into litter-strewn wastes. Surveys of tenants' attitudes in such estates reveal that quality of environment is an important issue to them.

Monumental and historic structures within the inner city must be retained as keys which reveal the symbolic significance of the place. Almost all of them are also tangible resources which could fulfil useful roles and enrich the lives of their users. Redundant board schools could house workshops and arts and social facilities. A school of this type in Cardiff has become a nationally-known arts centre. Modest refurbishments can make mills and factories suitable for small businesses. Leeds did some pioneering work in this field in the early 1970s but seems to have lost interest since. Churches and chapels could become major local centres, housing a variety of uses, including libraries, day centres, crèches and nursery schools. A church which is too large for one congregation to maintain might be shared by two or three.

Social change does not need to be the ruin of the inner city. Immigrants and students have brought a new vitality to some areas of Leeds. One cheering development in recent years has been the success of the independent University/Polytechnic student housing trust, UNIPOL, which provides accommodation in shared flats in converted buildings. UNIPOL has already rescued several listed buildings from dereliction. Both Belle Vue House (c. 1790) and All Souls Vicarage in Blackman Lane (1885) had been in a state of chronic disrepair. Belle Vue House now provides a home for twenty students; the vicarage, currently under restoration, will house a similar number. Other conversion schemes are being considered. UNIPOL's achievement is to marry resources (buildings) to needs (people). It sounds simple enough yet seems all too often to be beyond the powers of the local authority, the Church and other official bodies.

Official planning policies frequently seem designed to constrict human activities within approved boundaries. The 'obsolete' property which once housed countless small workshops and factories in and around the city centre was ruthlessly cleared. No provision was made to rehouse most of these businesses. But despite the long-term effects of such policies, it is these businesses which are responsible for regenerating parts of the city. The once-derelict Canal Basin area is being rapidly revived, with refurbished railway arches in great demand by small firms, and a number of buildings in the riverside area have recently been refurbished.

Inner-city Leeds needs more people, more activity, more diversity – in short, a reversal of the trends deliberately encouraged by post-war planning. Its existing fabric can provide an exciting and workable environment for living, working and leisure. The rot in Leeds can be stopped. But the continuing trend towards suburbanization must be halted. There are large areas of vacant land within the city, yet a huge housing development is planned on the very edge of the Temple Newsam estate, on valuable farm land. The fight against such schemes is not just a battle for the green belt but a part of the battle for the inner city. Woodhouse and Cross Green, Burley and Burmantofts, are still living communities, rich in history and tradition. Their survival is a matter of vital importance for the future of Leeds, which is, like all cities, the sum of its parts.

FURTHER READING

Beresford, Maurice. 'The Back-to-Back House in Leeds: 1787-1937', in S. D. Chapman (ed.), *The History of Working Class Housing*. Newton Abbot: David & Charles, 1971, pp. 93-132; and 'The Face of Leeds, 1780-1914', in Derek Fraser (ed.), *A History of Modern Leeds*. Manchester: Manchester University Press, 1980, pp. 72-112. Outstanding work on the historical development of the urban landscape of Leeds, including its housing patterns and the persistence of the back-to-back, of which the last were built in Kirkstall in 1937.

Betjeman, John. 'Leeds: a City of Contrasts', in his *First and Last Loves,* London: John Murray, 1952, pp. 30-38; Arrow Books, 1960, pp. 38-46. A perceptive and witty account of pre-war Leeds and its society by a pioneer appreciator of the positive qualities of industrial towns.

Finnigan, Robert. 'Housing Policy in Leeds between the Wars', in Joseph Melling (ed.), *Housing, Social Policy and the State*. London: Croom Helm, 1980, pp. 113-38. The social and political background of the 1930s clearances.

Hoggart, Richard. *The Uses of Literacy: Aspects of Working-Class Life, with Special Reference to Publications and Entertainment*. London: Chatto & Windus, 1957; paperback, Harmondsworth: Pelican, 1958. This classic contains an account of Hoggart's own upbringing in inner-city Leeds.

Jacobs, Jane. *The Death and Life of Great American Cities*. New York: Random House, 1961; Harmondsworth: Pelican, 1965. Classic American analysis of inner-city decay, as relevant to Leeds as to Los Angeles.

Leeds Community Housing Working Party. *Gradual Renewal in Leeds*

(1976); *House Sense* (1980). The LCHWP approach favours the retention and improvement of older housing, with new housing, where necessary, slotted into the existing urban fabric.

Linstrum, Derek. *Historic Architecture of Leeds*. Newcastle-on-Tyne: Oriel Press, 1969. A well-illustrated survey of the city's historic buildings.

Lloyd, David, and Powell, Ken. 'Leeds: Ancient and Modern', *Built Environment,* Vol. 3 (1977), pp. 232-7. Conservation and development in the city centre.

Pahl, R. E. 'Whose City?', in his *Whose City? and Other Essays on Sociology and Planning.* London: Longmans, 1970, pp. 201-8; Harmondsworth: Penguin, 1975. Discusses the limitations of the city planner.

Powell, Ken. 'The Fate of Some Churches in Leeds', *Yorkshire Architect,* Issue 52 (Jan.-Feb. 1977), pp. 6-10. The destruction of inner-city churches is linked with the replanning of the city.

Priestley, J. B. *English Journey*. London: Heinemann and Gollancz, 1934; Harmondsworth: Penguin, 1977. The eminent Yorkshire writer toured the country during the Depression, recording his impressions of places and people. He found Leeds generally depressing.

Ravetz, Alison. *Model Estate: Planned Housing at Quarry Hill, Leeds.* London: Croom Helm, 1974. Analyses the origins of the Quarry Hill Flats project, one of Britain's biggest inter-war housing schemes, and the reasons for its ultimate failure.

Ravetz, Alison. 'Changing Attitudes: the Idea of Value in the Inner City', *Built Environment,* Vol. 4 (1978), pp. 177-82. Describes the arbitrary way in which the role of the inner-city has been redefined.

Ravetz, Alison. 'Villages and Values', *Architects' Journal,* Vol. 169 (1979), pp. 1113-29. Describes one of the new out-of-town housing states and assesses its success as a community. Ravetz concludes that success is limited and that it is not easy to create new villages.

CHAPTER 9

The Relict Countryside: Preservation and Change in Suffolk

JOHN POPHAM

IN RECENT years, Suffolk's population has increased faster than that of East Anglia as a whole, which as a region has the fastest growth rate in England. The main reason for this is the startling rise in net inward migration, accounting for 74 per cent of total change between the years 1971 and 1973. Approximately one-quarter of this was 'planned migration' generated by the Greater London Council Town Development Act. Another quarter were people retiring to the Suffolk coast. Although growth has principally affected towns such as Haverhill and Bury St Edmunds, west Suffolk villages, in particular those centres where growth was encouraged in the past, have also sustained high growth rates.

Whereas 'planned' migrants may have shown little interest in their surroundings, the 'voluntary' migrants have sought out the attractive historic towns and villages. The historic centres of the settlements are often occupied by new-comers, with the indigenous population moving into new housing on the outskirts. In such cases, houses in the heart of the settlement command a premium.

The value people place on an historic environment can be gauged from a 1979 *Sunday Telegraph* estimate that property values in Lavenham were 25 per cent higher than in other Suffolk villages. Lavenham's distinction lies in being the most complete surviving small medieval town in eastern England; it contains entire streets of medieval buildings. About 1490, the town was ranked the four-teenth wealthiest in England — wealthier, for example, than York or Southampton, and perhaps comparable with the prosperity of, say, Leeds or Halifax in the nineteenth century. By 1550 Lavenham was in comparative decline, but since that time its residents have never been so wealthy that the town has been rebuilt to any extent (except a little in the nineteenth century) nor have they been so poor that property has fallen into total disrepair.

People looking round Lavenham today enjoy the mellow beauty of its remarkable buildings and the sense of continuity and stability they engender. The inhabitants have cared about this heritage for a considerable time: as long ago as 1911, the residents of Lavenham printed posters and called a public meeting to save a building threatened with demolition and removal. By the late 1930s outsiders were beginning to buy houses in the town in order to restore and retire to them. As early as 1944 the Suffolk Preservation Society — formed in 1929 largely to counter the appalling disfigurement of Suffolk's historic towns and villages by overhead electricity cables and ugly advertisement hoardings — commissioned a study of Lavenham jointly with the Society for the Protection of Ancient Buildings. Donald Insall's report, *Lavenham, Past, Present and Future*, appeared in 1961.

Throughout Suffolk newcomers and local families alike tend to feel closely involved in the affairs of the historic town or village in which they live. Many seek to promote preservation and to control development through one of the eighteen town or village amenity societies and the Suffolk Preservation Society. Architectural, planning and environmental causes are helped by the procedure for listing buildings of architectural or historic interest, the declaration of Conservation Areas, and the consultation process laid down by Town and County Planning legislation. At the scale of a market town or village such issues are in general easily comprehended; the effect of, say, the application of Structure Plan policy, guiding a county's future housing, employment and amenity needs, is likely to be fairly clear.

Views on the future of Suffolk's villages vary from place to place and among different sections of the community within a village. Most respondents to the consultation draft of the Structure Plan for the county felt that population growth through inward migration should be restricted as far as possible. However, many smaller settlements whose growth had previously been severely restricted requested a land allocation for the housing needs of the local community. Local employment growth was also felt to be essential to .he survival of the rural areas. On the other hand, experience had shown that a larger population did not prevent the continuing loss of retail shops, local transport, and other services. Many villages have in recent years doubled their population, yet the range of readily available services has declined.

Whereas the application of Structure Plan policy is likely to be fairly clear for any individual town, its impact on the county as a whole is much more complex. The Suffolk Preservation Society, having taken into account the views of individual members, formulated a comprehensive statement of the policies it wanted implemented. Professionally represented throughout most of the three-week public examination of the Structure Plan, it was thus able to put the case for conservation as effectively as the case which was made for industry and agriculture.

Preservation of the landscape poses more problems than that of buildings. The landscape of Suffolk is largely one of ancient enclosure; only 115 parishes out of a total of 500 have Parliamentary Enclosure Acts indicating landscape reorganization in the eighteenth and nineteenth centuries; of these, more than half were concerned exclusively with the enclosure of commons. The landscape of most of the county had evolved to its present form by late medieval or Tudor times. Ancient and sometimes high-banked hedges, with deep ditches running in sinuous lines along the sides of the lanes, still survive to show what much of Suffolk was like. High Suffolk, the clay plateau running through the centre of the county from south-west to north-east and occupying about two-thirds of its area, has been most affected by change. Its soil and gentle contours make it particularly suitable for large-scale arable farming, which has led to the loss of more than half of the historic landscape features in many parishes. Modern agriculture is not the only cause of loss. Forestry, building development and highway improvement also play a part.

Landscape features of historic importance include hedges and ditches forming parish boundaries (often of Anglo-Saxon origin), and bounding commons and greens, and the network of green lanes, some of which were once important highways. Unfortunately, the significance of many of these features is not apparent to the untrained eye, and most complaints about loss of landscape feature are made on visual grounds.

The lack of control over the removal of features from the landscape means that the countryside continues to be denuded both visually and historically. In Dedham Vale, one of Suffolk's Areas of Outstanding Natural Beauty, many of the existing landscape features recently recorded by the County Council will almost certainly disappear if an Anglian Water Authority scheme to improve the river Stour proceeds, enabling large areas of land to be tile-drained and converted from pasture to arable.

In the Suffolk Coast and Heaths Area of Outstanding Natural Beauty, the draft management plan for the Heritage Coast forming part of the Area contains no policies for conserving the landscape itself. In the absence of controls, heath continues to be ploughed up, water meadow continues to be converted into arable, and saltings and reed marsh continue to decline in area as drainage is improved. The lack of any record of existing features makes it impossible to determine when further losses should no longer be permitted or to select the most important features within each category for retention. The plan thus fails to protect the visual quality of the landscape — the sole reason for its designation as an Area of Outstanding Natural Beauty in the first place! As the Heritage Coast

Plan states, these features are 'non-renewable' resources, but under present legislation there is no satisfactory means of preventing their continued destruction. Each year, an increasing number of visitors to the coast look at a decreasing number of landscape features.

Churches and farm buildings are important elements in the landscape, both visually and historically. Suffolk has more than five hundred medieval churches, some of them now completely detached from their settlements. The survival of many is threatened by the enormous repair cost facing parishes with large decaying churches and small populations. Applications for redundancy will undoubtedly increase, although many parishes are making tremendous efforts to raise money for repairs. The Suffolk Historic Churches Trust, formed by the Suffolk Preservation Society in 1974, has already attracted 650 members who, largely by means of covenants and local authority funding, offered grants totalling £32,200 during 1979-80. It has also trained some forty volunteers to advise parishes in carrying out repairs.

While the fate of Suffolk's churches has aroused great public concern, the preservation of farm buildings has so far received less attention. As a result, many fine farm buildings and complete farmsteads are being lost. No proper survey of the county's farm buildings has been undertaken, and how many survive is not known. There is, therefore, no means of selecting those most worthy of preservation. With no control over demolition, except for the rare listed building or those in Conservation Areas, nothing can prevent further losses, which become more serious as fewer buildings survive. Even where a barn is listed, reluctance to include adjacent buildings for group value is marked, although retention is vital to understand properly the function of the buildings and to preserve visual unity.

It would, however, be untrue to say that concern about landscape and its features is lacking — the reverse is the case. At least half of the complaints and requests for help received by the Suffolk Preservation Society are about the landscape. Acting on such complaints is more difficult, however. Few people have a proper understanding of modern farming techniques, and few live in the countryside. There is no established machinery for dealing with landscape cases, by contrast with planning matters in which the local authority has power to act. In the absence of statutory controls, the Society must maintain a range of informal contacts to have any influence in matters affecting landscape. Cases may be taken up through the Farming and Wildlife Advisory Group, but usually the landscape feature has already been destroyed by the time the matter is reported.

Education provides another approach. The Suffolk Preservation Society instituted evening classes in 1976 to encourage members and others to survey their parish landscapes. Participants produced parish landscape plans recording the remaining landscape elements, where possible identifying important features by reference to early surveys, tithe maps and other sources. In 1979 the course was repeated for teachers in the Mid-Suffolk area, where the County Council and the Countryside Commission have a New Agricultural Landscapes project for a group of six parishes. The Society aims to complete a landscape plan for every parish in the county, to draw the attention of landowners, occupiers and the public to the importance of surviving landscape features.

It is often said that conflict over countryside conservation divides newcomers from indigenous members of the community. In reality the conflict is more often one between a farmer, industrialist or developer who proposes a scheme involving removal of landscape features, and the remainder of the community. Schemes advanced on grounds of increased food production or local employment are increasingly countered by a good case for conservation. When matters affecting the landscape — be they rights of way or loss of features — come up for discussion, a parish council often finds itself in some difficulty. In many councils, farming and landowning members are indifferent to conservation, and it can require much courage on the part of other members to oppose them. Many country-dwellers strongly averse to the present loss of landscape features are left feeling frustrated and helpless by the absence of statutory control and consultation procedures.

In the last few decades the nation's developing concern for its heritage has been expressed in legislation which has been gradually extended to give fairly comprehensive protection to historic towns, villages and buildings. Concern, however, is only translated into action when a strong enough voice demands it. More than half of the features of the Suffolk landscape have disappeared since 1945 — had more than half of the county's ten thousand listed buildings been demolished it is hard to believe that rapid action would not have been taken to prevent further loss. It still remains to convince Suffolk farmers and landowners that it is vitally important to preserve the more significant landscape features for historical, ecological and aesthetic reasons.

FURTHER READING

[Aldous, Tony.] 'Trend-setting Organisations: Suffolk Preservation Society', *Civic Trust News*, No. 79 (May/June 1980), pp. 2-3.

Buller, Henry, and Lowe, Philip. "The Environmentalists: The Council for the Protection of Rural England', *Vole*, Vol. 3, No. 9 (June 1980), pp. 32-5. Deals with the attitudes of Suffolk people to the landscapes they live in.

Jennings, Celia. *The Identity of Suffolk.* Lavenham: Suffolk Preservation Society, 1980. Sets the history of the Society in the context of Suffolk's development over the past half-century, and shows how feeling has responded to major environmental issues.

Scarfe, Norman. *Suffolk: A Shell Guide.* London: Faber & Faber, 1960; 3rd edition, 1976. The classic appreciative account, by an historically-oriented local observer, with an extensive gazetteer.

CHAPTER 10

Metroland: Half-Timbering and Other Souvenirs in the Outer London Suburbs

MATTHEW SAUNDERS

THIS CHAPTER is largely the story of the relationship between two parallel developments of the last century – the growth of the Outer London suburbs and the rise of the self-conscious conservation movement. Their respective debuts are the 1875 Housing Act, which is synonymous with byelaw housing, and the establishment of the Society for the Protection of Ancient Buildings in 1877. I chose Metroland because I live there, and more importantly because there has hardly ever been a match to its spectacular urban growth. Between 1918 and 1939, 618,971 houses were erected in Greater London, housing some 3 million people, the vast majority in the outer suburbs.

Literature has lampooned Suburban Man. It tells us that he has little civic as opposed to personal pride, is either incorrigibly philistine or conservative in matters of art and architecture, and prefers to endow his urban life with spurious rural overtones, living in pseudo-Tudor houses with half-timbered gables, inglenooks and cartwheel gates. However, the gentle propaganda of Betjeman and others has softened this caricature. Nicholas Taylor in *The Village in the City* (1973), following a path pioneered by Sir James Richards's *Castles on the Ground* (1946), has provided an impressive intellectual defence of so-called suburban architectural values. I hope to show that the Outer London suburbs are no longer devoid of a feeling for architecture, if they ever were so. The more roguish Victorian architecture and the unremittingly 'modern' are still beyond the pale, but sympathy with nearly all other periods and

165

styles is now well entrenched.

This was not always so. We just have to count the demolitions. As the half-million houses were going up, priceless treasures were coming down – very often as a direct consequence. One small area of North London in the 1920s saw the demolition of Hornsey parish church except for the tower in 1927, Enfield Palace – a home of Elizabeth I as princess – in 1928, and the Edmonton house where John Keats was apprenticed, in 1931. Mansions were broken up at an appalling rate. It is my estimate that in the present London boroughs of Enfield and Haringey the equivalent of three Grade I and 17 Grade II* buildings were demolished in the two dreadful decades of the twenties and thirties, a record worse than that for England as a whole in the last five years. Bexley had six great houses of note in 1930, only three by 1936. But two important qualifications must be made. First, the arrival of the suburbs gave many historic buildings a new lease on life, saving them from demolition by conversion to offices or clubhouses. Most such 'conservation' was fortuitous rather than conscious, demolition being regarded as simply wasteful rather than distasteful; but there was certainly some desire to retain beauty for its own sake. Second, there is little evidence that contemporary attitudes towards historic buildings in the countryside were any more sensitive. At the same time as Enfield Palace was destroyed, the rococo splendour of Nuthall Temple in Nottingham-shire, for example, was being smashed to pieces.

Attitudes since then have considerably improved. But the post-war conservation movement as reflected in the Outer London suburbs has two quite distinct aspects. One is conservation by reaction: the wish, born of distaste for the drabness and uniformity of many suburbs, to preserve historic pre-suburban remains, the buildings which represent the now urbanized villages and country towns. The other is a positive appreciation of suburban character and design, of the buildings erected during the great suburban expansions. Both, particularly the first, are to some extent indebted to the Society for the Protection of Ancient Buildings. After all, William Morris's resolve to preserve ancient buildings was forged in his youth at Water House, Walthamstow, as he watched that quiet Essex town transformed into what is now one of the most dispiriting of suburbs. The second aspect, too, owes something to the inception of the SPAB, the suburbs at their best being the Indian summer of the Arts and Crafts Movement, of which the SPAB is one of the longest-lived offspring.

The first trend is the most powerful. Most suburbs have little distinctive sense of place – the archetypal semi is as much at home in, say, north-east England as in London. Despite its pretensions to historic appearance, the suburb usually owes nothing to the genuine vernacular of the area. Reaction against the spread of uniform suburbia fostered a desire to preserve historic buildings threatened by it. Some of the earliest public purchases of such buildings were made specifically to protect them from the threat of demolition or envelopment posed by suburban growth. For example, the 1878 purchase of Epping Forest by the City of London Corporation included the so-called Queen Elizabeth's Hunting Lodge in Chingford, to be preserved 'as an object of public and antiquarian interest' (Epping Forest Act 1878). In Twickenham, the delightful Palladian villa of Marble Hill was acquired in 1902 by the London County Council, after a prior sale to a developer had provoked strong local opposition. At the turn of the century most London boroughs acquired an historic house for use as a museum. Ruislip was one of the first local authorities to use powers bestowed by the Housing and Town Planning Act of 1909, designed to safeguard historic character, which it applied to the protection of Eastcote.

The twentieth-century suburban desire to mix urban life with rural residences was thus not an alien notion. In the eighteenth century as well as in the twentieth, 'urban' developments attempted to preserve 'rural' pre-urban reminders, natural or architectural. The pattern of supplementing rather than replacing, of respecting the historic core and building round it, had also been common in pre-nineteenth-century village expansion around London – in a way, a practical expression of the Picturesque. Fashionable eighteenth-century developments often centred on ancient greens and commons, as at Wimbledon and Kew and, farther out, at Monken Hadley and Edmonton.

At Edmonton the Green was built up without any urban flavour. Just as Batty Langley had spoken in his *Principles of Gardening* (1728) of the visual pleasure found 'in orchards, haystacks and woodpiles', those constructing houses around Edmonton Green in the eighteenth century preserved its rural appearance as far as they could. Most residents were 'of the middling sort' not engaged directly in agriculture, but eighteenth- and nineteenth-century deeds clearly show the continuing mass of farm buildings around the houses, 'granaries, stables, bullock pounds, sheep pens and orchards'. A print of 1806 shows the centre of the Green taken up by a large pond.

What differentiated nineteenth- and twentieth-century suburbia from its antecedents was an element of fantasy, the harking after the sentimental and the quaint. The fashion of half-timbering, coinciding with the taste for exposing genuine timber frames in East Anglia by the removal of later renders, did lead to excesses. In 1923 half-timbering was actually applied to the Georgian Broomfield House at Palmers Green – then a museum – in an attempt to make an eighteenth-century building appear sixteenth-century. In 1859 a conical fairytale cover was placed over Tottenham Well just as the well went out of use. At Southgate, the sheepfold was preserved among semis in the 1930s, its bucolic echoes emphasized by the small 'Woodman' Inn opposite. At Enfield a quite extraordinary castle arose about 1880, known as Denby Dene, on the London Road. Most suburban streets and pubs were given rural names. The spine road through North London is still called Green Lanes – a pre-suburban name which has 'stuck'. Others were knowingly anachronistic when dubbed Sylvan Avenue, The Dell, etc.; similarly with the pubs, the

Hop Poles, the Wheatsheaf, the Plough. Sentimental attachment, rather than an intellectual appreciation of fine architecture, still pervades the 'Notes' in many suburban newspapers, strong in preservationist spirit of the Good Old Days variety.

Examples of this first strand of suburban conservation, the preservation of pre-suburban remains, are abundant. A classic in this category is St Mary's church, Perivale. Villagey in size, materials and character, this delightful little building, a golf course on one side, the dual carriageways of Western Avenue fifty yards on the other, pulls at the heartstrings of the citizens of Ealing. Following redundancy when it was proposed to sell it for private conversion in 1977, a group of local 'Friends' protested and have since taken it over for concerts and exhibitions. Kingsbury Old Church, largely of the thirteenth century, has similarly been taken over by the Wembley Historical Society. The church was retained when a replacement, in fact a church bodily moved from Wells Street in central London, was erected nearby in 1847. The same juxtaposition recurred a few years later at Stoke Newington when Gilbert Scott provided a new parish church but did not demolish the old. Here, as at Kingsbury, the contrast was unmistakeably between a town and a village church. The decision to retain the old was consciously made to conserve the focal point of the pre-suburban village despite the consequent burden of having to maintain two adjacent buildings.

Brentford's parish church of St Lawrence tells a different tale. At first, the town displayed almost complete lack of feeling for its oldest building, a structure which through its many monuments encapsulated the historic identity of the area over four centuries. The church, fifteenth-century in its tower, eighteenth-century in its nave, fell into disuse in 1961 and for the next fifteen years was subjected to wretched vandalism. Now, however, thanks to a campaign by the local New Hope Theatre Company, conversion into a community centre and theatre is well advanced.

In Bush Hill Park, Enfield, a vain but determined fight was mounted to preserve the cottage orné – 'Enfield's last thatched building' – that served as the lodge to the local golf club. Thatch, redolent of the country and 'crafts', is so loaded with extra-architectural connotations that its presence alone seemed to convince many of the need for retention. In King's Road, Tottenham, an early-nineteenth-century farmhouse was saved from demolition by the local historical society and now sits uneasily in the midst of a soul-less council estate, a disorientated point of historical reference. In Southgate the proposed redevelopment of the Georgian cottages at Nos 23-32 The Green led directly to the foundation of the local Civic Trust.

In Hayes, where hardly anything of historic interest survives, local concern has by default concentrated on a simple farmhouse at 212 Church Road, all that Hayes has to remind it of its rural origins. Arguments over its fate have raged for years. The farmhouse now lies derelict and the local council wishes to rebuild in facsimile. The local historical society quite rightly fears the consequent loss of authenticity. Architecturally it is a poor specimen, but historically to Hayes it means everything.

In the early sixties a scheme to drive an unneeded relief road through Enfield churchyard was opposed by a petition signed by 12,000. This led to the founding of the Enfield Preservation Society which now has 2,000 members, ranking as one of the largest civic groups in the country.

The positive appreciation of suburbia is the second aspect of conservation I wish to treat. By its nature, it owes less to historical sentiment than to a cooler, although not necessarily more esoteric, appreciation of 'good' architecture and skilful design. A love of architecture is backed by a strong communal will to conserve in Hampstead Garden Suburb. There is the usual apparatus of control from above: fairly extensive listing, with the Institute which provides the cultural centre being listed Grade I, and most of the Suburb designated as a Conservation Area, with the central core 'Outstanding'. The London Borough of Barnet exercises a tough policy of Development Control, precluding insensitive change. This is coupled with a considerable measure of grassroots acceptance. Local people organized a highly successful exhibition in 1975 entitled 'Suburb Heritage'. In the following years, a local study group invited the original architects to visit and issued as sane and as sensitive a design guide for the care of a given area as has been produced anywhere. Simultaneously an appeal for £40,000 was launched for St Jude's, Lutyens's great church at the hub of the Suburb, a large sum for a building put up as recently as 1908. (Twentieth-century churches in the 'unplanned' London suburbs have also successfully appealed for ambitious restoration programes. The church of St Stephen, Bush Hill Park, in Enfield, opened in 1919, has just completed a project of repair and cleaning at a cost of £13,000.)

It may come as a surprise that the pattern repeats itself in Muswell Hill, as much a byword for the staid suburban life of the Edwardian clerk as was Surbiton for that of the interwar middle class. Muswell Hill was lauded in the 1906 edition of *Where to Live Around London*:

It is one of the most salubrious heights around London for, standing at an elevation of over 400 feet above sea level, the air is exceptionally pure and it enjoys its full share of sunshine. This dominant height also commands extensive views over the Middlesex Vale with Epping Forest and the Hertfordshire Hills in the distance on one side and the heights of Hampstead and Highgate on the other. Its many residential thoroughfares are all of a pleasant character and contain numerous well-planned and artistic houses lying back beyond ample forecourt gardens.

This was estate agents' soft sell, designed to entice the city clerk and skilled artisans for whom the suburb was constructed in the first decade of this century. Now listen to the London Borough of Haringey planners who declared it a Conservation Area in 1973: 'Muswell Hill, the Broadway and residential environs are a remarkably well preserved example of an early Edwardian shopping centre (*c.* 1903) and *its completeness and townscape quality is probably unrivalled in any inland town'* (my italics). Words of praise which would have been quite impossible before 1970.

Even more surprisingly, in view of the myth that planners lead rather than follow public opinion, this interest was reflected among Muswell Hill residents. The catalyst was an application to demolish the former Presbyterian church in the Broadway, built in 1903 to the design of George Baines, who was selected after a competition judged by Charles Harrison Townsend, the distinguished Art Nouveau architect. Spotlisted at the second attempt, this extra-ordinary structure, built in flint and hard Ruabon brick, is the most distinctive landmark in the Hill. The threat to demolish it gave birth to BROACH, the Broadway Church Action Group, an offshoot of the residents' association, which campaigned, with the backing of the London Borough of Haringey, for the preservation of the church and its conversion into a concert hall. They won the public inquiry, an outcome helped by the personal appearance of Sir John Summerson and Felix Aprahamian, but owing most to a petition signed by no less than 9,000 of the 30,000 population of Muswell Hill.

People's need to feel some pride in their surroundings can project itself onto buildings which art historians still tend to dismiss, a dismissal which prompts the Department of the Environment to follow suit. The DoE lists some buildings in the London suburbs to the stupefaction of most of the locals — Holden's Piccadilly Underground stations, for example ('Southgate's Stately Tube', said the local paper over an article consisting mainly of street interviews with uniformly indifferent commuters). The unfortunate corollary is a refusal to list buildings for which there is a local feeling but which happen to be of a date or in a style not in academic favour. Ilford Town Hall and Alexandra Palace are the classic examples.

The exuberant Edwardian baroque Town Hall, built in 1899, is the best building in the High Street — yet the DoE rejected local calls for its listing. Alexandra Palace, 'Ally Pally' to North Londoners, is a huge People's Palace of

172

1875 built to answer South London's Crystal Palace. If ever a building was a landmark this is it, but the DoE refuse to list, on the principle that size cannot compensate for banality. This despite the fact that the DoE lists buildings for their 'interest', not their merit. Government neglect of 'Ally Pally' is the sadder because of considerable local feeling for it. When the Palace was first threatened a grassroots association grew up to fight for it. A referendum conducted by the GLC in 1974 cast an overwhelming local vote in favour of retention. (The Palace was severely damaged by fire in 1980. A definite decision on its future is awaited although the intention to rebuild has been announced by the Council.)

The wish to conserve can be inspired as much by purely sentimental and often whimsical nostalgia as by an intellectual appreciation of architectural design and a sense of civic pride. It is because of the combination of these two forces that a study of conservation in the Outer London suburbs is so interesting. Through the admittedly fortuitous circumstance of their greatest development having been between the world wars, appreciation even of 'modern' architecture is being pioneered now in such areas, as the Secretary of State lists outstanding structures of the twenties and thirties, buildings like Sutton Baptist Church and Hornsey Town Hall. It is indeed heartily refreshing that good architecture, be it historic or modern, can find defenders among Suburban Man, and that the destruction of the principal part of the façade of the Firestone factory on the Great West Road in Hounslow in 1980, on the eve of its listing, can be regarded as a national outrage, provoking not just a ministerial statement and an editorial in the *Daily Telegraph* but local anger too.

FURTHER READING

Dyos, H. J. *Victorian Suburb: A Study of the Growth of Camberwell*. Leicester: Leicester University Press, 1961, reprinted 1973. A classic monograph on the mid- and late-nineteenth-century development of a single Inner London suburb.

Locality, Community and Conservation

Jackson, Alan A. *Semi-Detached London: Suburban Development, Life and Transport, 1900-39*. London: Allen and Unwin, 1973. The classic book on the growth of the Outer London suburbs.

Jenkins, Simon. *The Companion Guide to Outer London*. London: Collins, 1981.

Olsen, Donald J. *The Growth of Victorian London*. London: Batsford, 1976. A broad canvas mainly applying to the inner London area.

Richards, James M. *The Castles on the Ground: The Anatomy of Suburbia,* with illustrations by John Piper. London: Architectural Press, 1946; John Murray, 1973. A witty and original essay.

Taylor, Nicholas. *The Village in the City*. London: Maurice Temple Smith, 1973. A dazzling polemic against the false gods of modern planning, with a powerful defence of suburban planning.

Part IV

THE FUTURE OF OUR HERITAGE

HOW CAN we reconcile the desire to preserve the past with other needs? Preservation costs money, and as Max Hanna and Elisabeth Beazley here remind us, the costs mount with increasing attention and attendance. The more people are enticed to view historic sites and artifacts and to inhabit older buildings, the more must be invested in protecting, rehabilitating, and displaying them.

The dilemma is in one sense more apparent than real, for revenue from visitors and purchasers could help to defray these costs. But heritage ownership and management often make for an inequitable allocation of costs and benefits. For example, tax receipts from general spending by foreign visitors who tour Britain's historic houses, cathedrals, and other ancient monuments in no way contribute to maintain these structures, nor do conservation grants relate to such income.

Conservation costs deserve to be balanced against other benefits, too. Maintaining and renovating older buildings saves substantial amounts of energy and raw materials that would otherwise have to be used to replace them with new structures. In the United States, such re-use of the heritage not only caters for historic, aesthetic, and associational needs but is demonstrably cost-effective. In Britain, by contrast, current tax policies penalize the conservation of older buildings — notably the 15 per cent value-added tax put on repairs but not on new construction. A pronounced bias among property valuers, mortgagers, and banks against older structures also inhibits their conversion and re-use.

Many key figures in British government and industry continue to view conservation as a burden on the economy, an obstacle to progress. Marcus Binney traces this bias back to post-war faith in a brave new world. Conservation costs do fall heavily on some small communities, like Ely, Wells and Beverley, which must devote a substantial proportion of local resources and skills to maintain cathedrals that ought to be supported as part of the national heritage. But the preservation-linked benefits already noted in connection with tourism, energy supplies, and raw materials show how groundless are fears that preservationists will take up a huge proportion of the nation's resources.

Preservation's ultimate rationale lies beyond such economic benefits, however. It is the less tangible realms of national identity and personal connection with the past which give our material heritage its major value. These attributes cannot be quantified. But they enrich the environment and the quality of life, and animate the entire preservation movement.

The growth of public interest in the past, notably of visits to historic places, threatens the very fabric that sustains these values. As Max Hanna shows for English cathedrals, tourists not only erode the heritage they have come to see, but may endanger its physical survival. Caretakers must be constantly vigilant against theft and vandalism. Similar problems apply to prehistoric antiquities and to country houses whose management Elisabeth Beazley discusses.

Vigilance and funding can solve most of the physical problems engendered by an increasingly popular heritage. But the loss of ambience, the impact of crowd pollution on historical experience itself, is less easily dealt with. Thronged by thousands daily, Stonehenge and Canterbury Cathedral can no longer be seen or experienced as they once were. In cathedrals, the press of visitors subverts the vital atmosphere of contemplative awe and tends to drive out the religious community, the cathedrals' essential *raison d'être.* Many cathedrals are reluctant to charge admission, Hanna notes, because of the degeneration of function such fees imply. But the sale of postcards, guidebooks, and souvenirs can likewise detract from the atmosphere as do tour guides, photography, and minatory signs and barriers.

For historic sites with plenty of space, Beazley re-commends other solutions. Counter-attractions can entice away those visitors to historic houses and gardens less interested in antiquity than activity. Ancillary structures and attractions need not intrude on historical features. All the same, a rising demand for heritage must be accommo-dated within a finite supply of historic sites and artifacts, however broadly history is defined. While 'pleasing decay' remains a valuable component of our experience of the past, neither the Tower of London nor Madame Tussaud's suffices to meet every historical taste. To cater for the sense of discovery as well as for the familiar, some heritage sites should be left difficult of access and devoid of interpretive paraphernalia. As Beazley notes, we are some-times better off temporarily lost than over-informed.

The choice we all face, Binney suggests, is between a real and a contrived past. Continuing destruction coupled with growing public interest not only enhance the scarcity value of actual relics, but stimulate their imitation and replication. In the United States newly-constructed historic villages may soon outnumber extant survivals, and antiquities are apt to be moved and restored rather than left *in situ*. The same tendencies are also transforming the tangible past in Britain and elsewhere.

Imitations of antiquity may have many merits, but they can no more replace the real thing than reproduction furniture can replace true antiques. Far more than actual artifacts preserved from the past, such facsimiles bear the traits of our own time — a problem explored at greater length in the Conclusion. The essays in Part IV show that problems of conservation, access, and interpretation, along with those of destruction and neglect, become increasingly acute with growing public interest in our material heritage.

177

CHAPTER 11

Cathedrals at Saturation Point?

MAX HANNA

A NINETEENTH-CENTURY Precentor of Chichester Cathedral
once wrote that cathedrals 'are the history of England
written in stone; the erection, not of ecclesiastics only, but
of every class of the community; storehouses and treasuries
of the arts, whether in glass, architecture, paintings,
sculpture, or carved work'. Such an immense heritage must
largely explain the huge numbers of people now visiting
cathedrals. The impact of visitors on cathedrals in England
was surveyed by the English Tourist Board during 1977 and
1978, and recommendations for action published in *English
Cathedrals and Tourism* (1979) were devised with advice from
representatives of the Deans and Provosts Conference, the
Cathedral Architects Conference, the Cathedrals Advisory
Committee, and the Church of England Guild of Vergers.

It is possible that as many as twenty million visits, yearly,
are made to cathedrals and greater churches, such as
Westminster Abbey, in England alone. During the first
fortnight in August 1978 over a million people were
counted (not including worshippers) visiting a sample of
twenty-six cathedrals. 17,132 people visited York Minster
on one day. Virtually every cathedral and greater church in
a sample of 39 (out of 90 in England) increased the number
of its visitors over the past ten years. The less well-known
cathedrals experienced the fastest increases, the famous
cathedrals more modest ones: Rochester a 500 per cent
growth in ten years, Norwich a 100 per cent growth. These
increases have been fuelled partly by a rapid growth of
foreign tourism. An ETB survey of visitors to eleven
cathedrals in August 1978 found that the proportion of

178

foreigners varied from 60 per cent at St Paul's to 16 per cent at Lichfield Cathedral.

Answering the question posed in the title of this chapter is not a simple matter owing to the subjective nature of the concept of saturation, or congestion. One man's bothersome crowd may be another man's happy throng. Many tourists seem to prefer congregating in large numbers to exploring in solitude. However, the types of pressure increasingly being exerted on cathedrals cannot be tolerated in the same way as they might be on popular beaches or beauty spots. Cathedrals are primarily places of worship. Also the architecture, atmosphere, and other features of interest in cathedrals cannot be properly appreciated unless there is a reasonable relationship between the number of visitors and the space available.

Interviews with cathedral authorities and an hourly count of visitors have enabled the English Tourist Board, to some extent, to measure the degree of congestion in thirty-three cathedrals and six greater churches. Thirteen of these buildings, or one third, suffer from some degree of congestion. Among the most congested cathedrals are Canterbury, Coventry, Durham, St Paul's and York Minster. At Canterbury 'the nave and choir become congested with visitors during July and August. Total saturation is now being reached much of the time and the atmosphere of the Cathedral is thereby spoiled.' Coventry Cathedral reports that 'considerable disruption is caused, particularly by parties', Durham that 'pressure on the West End tends to be considerable during the summer months when special services are in progress', St Paul's that 'queues form waiting to go down the crypt and up into the galleries, and congestion occurs in bottlenecks, at peak times', and York that 'the worst period is probably during the first two weeks of July when particularly large numbers of school children come to the Minster'. As long ago as 1970 a survey of Westminster Abbey by Binder, Hamlyn, and Fry estimated that the 'comfort level' of 35 square feet of open floor area per person was exceeded more than half of the time. On

179

14 Canterbury Cathedral with visitors, midday, August 1978

15 Canterbury Cathedral: wear on the Dean's Steps

many occasions the number of visitors within the Abbey swelled to nearly 3,000. This represents an average density of 8 square feet per person. During these periods the consultants could not complete their measurements because of the difficulties of moving round the Abbey, and they commented that 'the noise, heat, congestion, and delays associated with this number of visitors has to be experienced for its full impact to be appreciated'. Since 1970 the number of visitors has certainly increased.

At some cathedrals and greater churches only specific parts of the building are subject to congestion. For example, there is the popular giftshop at Norwich Cathedral, the cramped library, and its circular staircase, at Salisbury Cathedral, and the area near the Becket window at Oxford Cathedral – a favourite spot for the tourist guides. At Wells Cathedral, which has been described as the 'largest free umbrella in the West', people have difficulty in getting in and out at the west door on rainy days during the summer.

The August 1978 count of visitors revealed that weekdays, particularly Tuesdays and Wednesdays, are even busier than weekends, and that the busiest period is between 2 and 4 p.m. The period between 2 and 3 p.m. is, generally, more than four times as crowded as the quietest open hour (9-10 a.m.). At Chichester and St Alban's the peak hour was more than ten times as busy as the quietest hour. At some of the more popular cathedrals the number of visitors is considerable even at off-peak times. At St Paul's, for example, the peak average hourly flow is 2,470 (at 2-3 p.m.), but between 9 and 10 a.m. the average hourly flow is as high as 550, and between 5 and 6 p.m. it is 870. The highest recorded hourly rate of arrivals was 2,952 between 1 and 2 p.m. on Thursday, 3 August, at York Minster. At St Paul's the highest number was 2,862 and at Canterbury 2,570. Each of these three cathedrals receives almost as many peak-hour visitors as does the Tower of London at its very busiest hour.

Thus it can be concluded that a few cathedrals, some of the time, are at saturation point and that an increasing number of cathedrals and greater churches are suffering from congestion in vulnerable spaces.

The means various cathedrals are using to ease congestion include the introduction of recommended routes, the removal of chairs, a 'green light' system restricting access to specified numbers of visitors at a time, and a quota controlling the timing of coach parties. There is scope for wider use of these methods, and in some cases more stringent controls should be considered. In particular, cathedral authorities might introduce an admission charge during the peak season, ensuring that the charge is sufficiently high to be an effective deterrent. Experience at Salisbury Cathedral, which has been charging for admission since 1974, suggests that an entry charge also reduces the amount of improper behaviour and improves the atmosphere in the Cathedral. During the peak tourist months, visitors vastly outnumber the worshippers, who should be admitted free by a separate door. At present charges are made for entry to parts of many cathedrals, but this merely increases congestion by causing the formation of queues. By charging admission for the cathedral as a whole these queues would be diverted to the exterior of the building where they are less disruptive.

Whether or not cathedral authorities decide to charge for admission it is advisable for them to draw up a policy for coach tour operators and other organized groups of visitors. Coach parties take much advantage of the free access to cathedrals and make little or no financial contribution in return. They perhaps feel that entrance to the building has been paid for as part of the tour itself. It might be argued that it is inequitable to charge parties whilst not similarly charging individuals, but individuals are less disruptive, and have a higher propensity to make donations and to buy souvenirs, not being subject to the tight schedules of the tour operators. Charging parties would enable the cathedral authorities to manage their arrival times so as to avoid religious services, peak visiting times, or the simultaneous arrival of several groups. Further control could be arranged through the issue of licences to tour operators.

However, congestion within cathedral buildings is not the only problem caused by the massive increase in cathedral tourism. The problem most frequently mentioned by eighteen respondents, 46 per cent of the total, was the inadequacy of parking facilities for visitors during the summer season. This problem, for the most part, is outside the control of the ecclesiastical authorities. Few cathedrals have car park facilities which can be used by visitors, and local authority car parks are often too far away or too small.

One of the worst parking situations is to be found at Wells. The Dean and Chapter have no control over the road beside the cathedral, which has a two-hour waiting restriction and gets very crowded. There is no large car park nearby. It can be difficult to find parking near the cathedral even in winter. The problem is at its worst during flower festivals when hundreds of coaches converge on Wells. In Oxford there are no parking facilities near the cathedral, and this causes traffic problems in the road outside Christ Church College, while coaches stop temporarily to drop or pick up their parties. At Salisbury, despite parking space for ten coaches at a time, there is periodically complete congestion in the Close. Coaches may have only thirty-five minutes to spare for the cathedral and try to take short cuts, causing a blockage. More parking facilities could be provided within some cathedral precincts, but only at the cost of spoiling the appearance and peaceful charm of such areas. The atmosphere of the Close at Salisbury would be much improved if visitors were banned from parking within the precincts. Parking facilities can probably be improved only through liaison with the responsible local authorities. Assistance in the provision of toilets would also be much appreciated. Local authorities, after all, benefit from the rates paid by establishments dependent on the tourism and spending generated by cathedral visits.

Another problem causing concern to the cathedral authorities (and their architects) is the wear and tear attributed to visitors, mentioned by thirteen respondents (33 per cent). Mainly affected are steps, paving stones, and memorials inserted into floors. Most examples given of visitor damage were fairly minor in nature, but at a few buildings the problem has reached serious proportions.

Two of the worst affected are Canterbury Cathedral and St George's Chapel, Windsor. The Surveyor of Canterbury Cathedral reported that the stone floor of the nave and various steps are particularly susceptible to visitor wear and tear. Stones under the tower are being eroded at an alarming rate. Paving in softer parts of the Portland stone in the south aisle has been worn away to a depth of 1¼ inches. The Victorian Dean's Steps as well as the medieval steps to the site of the shrine of St Thomas à Becket are badly worn. In the Trinity Chapel, a stone has been lost from a mosaic in a roundel in the floor. In the south-west transept, which is the main sales area in the cathedral, the inscriptions on the floor are beginning to disappear and some are now unreadable. In the Martyrdom the edges of the brass fittings are being worn smooth. Visitors cannot now be allowed into the Bell Harry Tower because of wear on the roof leading. The medieval wall surface beside the north stairs from the crypt has been marked with graffiti and many walls, piers, and columns, where people can touch them, are very dirty. Despite a strong wrought-iron railing, small fragments of Henry IV's tomb have been broken off, and it has been necessary to erect a perspex screen as a temporary first-aid measure. The handrail up to the choir has been broken as a result of children swinging on it. Outside the cathedral, a plastic barrier protecting the grass in the Close was subjected to such pressures that it had to be replaced by a metal one.

At St George's Chapel the architect reports:

The floor has suffered to the point where much of it now needs replacement. The nave floor was laid in the 1780s and is of Portland stone, some of it now barely ½ inch thick. Dusting-up as it does, at an alarming rate, it is very difficult to keep anything in the building free of dust. The heating system doesn't help –

16 St George's Chapel, Windsor: the shop

17 Salisbury Cathedral parking: despite space for ten coaches, the
Close periodically suffers complete congestion

this is a gravity warm-air system and picks up the dust from the floor and deposits it on every ledge in the chapel. Some of the beautiful ledger-stones are becoming worn to illegibility and one or two which are in bas-relief are suffering very badly.

Vandalism is a problem in some cathedrals, but this is related less to the flow of visitors than to their location in areas of urban decay and associated social problems.

Current methods of preventing or minimizing wear and tear caused by visitors include rationing access, roping off or covering up valuable areas, the provision of felt overshoes, the use of replicas, and staff control. At Exeter Cathedral access to the tower is restricted to one party a week. The retro-choir at Winchester Cathedral has been roped off to prevent people treading on the medieval tiles – these were being ruined by stiletto heels, a fashion which, regrettably, is once again finding favour. In the choir at Wells Cathedral a rope prevents people from lifting up the delicate wooden misericords. However, a verger will show the misericords to visitors on request and a few are displayed in the south choir aisle. Overshoes are provided at the Chapter House of Westminster Abbey but are rather cumbersome and impracticable when visitors are numerous. At Salisbury Cathedral a replica of the Wyville brass is provided for rubbing purposes. At Norwich Cathedral the large cathedral staff on hand (including volunteers) help to keep vandalism to a minimum. Staff can also help to prevent unintentional damage. These protective measures should be more widely adopted to safeguard fabric most at risk.

Litter was a problem mentioned by twelve respondents (31 per cent), mainly at cathedrals with a lawned close. At Canterbury, where the problem is most acute, the rubbish left in the precincts fills three skips every week during the summer. This costs £40 in hire charges excluding the labour of collection. The skips themselves damage the gateway by scoring it. The gardener at Exeter Cathedral has to clear up litter from the Close twice a day in the summer, and in the picnic area near the coffee room at Norwich Cathedral a man has to be employed to tidy up. As regards interiors, the verger of St George's Chapel, Windsor, reports that tourist litter causes a great problem for the cleaning staff; at Lichfield Cathedral there are complaints of ice creams causing stains on the floor; at Oxford discarded flash bulbs and stubbed-out cigarettes are left lying about; and at York one of the main problems is the quantity of chewing gum trodden into the paving.

Coach parties are a very common sight in cathedrals. Some tour operators and their guides were criticized by thirteen respondents (33 per cent), mainly for disturbing religious services, giving wrong information, and rushing their parties round too quickly, but also for bad manners and causing congestion. A former Dean of Salisbury Cathedral has written of occasional

trouble with guides from tourist agencies when they bring parties to the Cathedral and find that a service is in progress – quite possibly a service which takes up much of the interior of the building. Usually the guides are sensible and take their party round the other buildings such as the Chapter House until the service is ended. But sometimes they behave rather inconsiderately and insist on taking their party through the building and making clearly audible commentaries which disturb the congregation. Also, licensed guides with parties from London have been heard to give inaccurate information about the Cathedral. For example, a party of Americans was recently told by their guide that English cathedrals were the possession of the National Trust and religious services did not take place in them except very rarely on special occasions, and the famous spire was built in the 16th century by Sir Christopher Wren.

Some cathedrals with a large number of their own guides have imposed restrictions on commercial guides. Tour operators have to use Canterbury Cathedral's authorized voluntary guides, and at Exeter Cathedral only two tour operators have been authorized by the Dean and Chapter to do their own guiding. The touting for guided tours outside the West Front at Exeter has now been stopped. The only people apart from Abbey staff permitted to lecture groups of visitors within Westminster Abbey are approved London Tourist guides. At Ely Cathedral, where resident guides are available free of charge, tour operators must obtain advance permission if they wish to use their own guides.

Whereas commercial guides tend to treat cathedrals as museums, resident guides will stress their religious significance. Thus, ideally, the cathedrals should train and provide all their guides themselves. This would become more feasible if cathedrals were to charge for guided tours, which are now mainly free, thereby building up their professional resources. Alternatively, cathedral authorities could examine the commercial guides, restricting access to those who achieve the required standard. A meeting at the beginning of each season could bring all certified guides up to date on new developments in the cathedral.

Other problems often referred to were pilfering, noise, and unruly behaviour. At Bath Abbey, pilfering from the bookstall cost between £700 and £1,000 a year until the current practice of manning the door was introduced. Canterbury Cathedral is a major sufferer from pilferage, partly because its two giftshops are so congested. Pilferage extends beyond souvenirs to books of common prayer (at Oxford) and a choir stall embroidery (at Wells). Noise is a particular problem at Canterbury Cathedral where visitor numbers are so great that the noise at times reaches intolerable levels, interfering with the work of cathedral officers and interrupting choir practice. Unruly behaviour appears to emanate mainly from school parties and French teenagers. Proximity to language schools increases the French teenager problem, as at Chichester.

Another problem is the difficulty of finding suitable sites for such visitor facilities as giftshops and refectories. Commercial criteria suggest that such facilities should be prominently placed within the cathedral, but this may conflict with religious and aesthetic values. Also, new buildings constructed in the precincts may not blend harmoniously with their surroundings, yet the use of traditional building materials may be prohibitively expensive.

Cathedrals at Saturation Point?

At least two thirds of the cathedrals and greater churches seek to control visitor behaviour through the use of notices. The remainder rely largely on vergers to control unacceptable behaviour. However, many notices are probably read by only a minority of visitors because they tend to be written in small letters. The dilemma is that the large and obtrusive notices, increasingly required to communicate with more and more foreign visitors, also harm the cathedral's appearance, especially at the entrance. Whether or not notices are an effective means of controlling behaviour, they do indicate what gives ecclesiastical authorities cause for concern. At least sixteen cathedrals placed some form of restriction on photography. Mainly this takes the form of charging for a permit but also there are a few instances of an outright ban. Some prohibit flash photography, the removal of furniture, or the use of a tripod. Dogs, smoking, eating, drinking, and inappropriate dress are also frequently frowned upon.

Whilst this chapter is primarily concerned with the problems arising from the impact of twenty million visitors yearly, it should not be forgotten that there are also considerable benefits to the cathedrals, the visitors, and the economy both nationally and locally.

Visitors are making an increasingly important contribution towards the maintenance and repair costs of cathedrals and greater churches. Revenue from visitors is estimated to account for half of the total annual income of Coventry Cathedral, 47 per cent of that of York Minster, 42 per cent of Salisbury Cathedral, 40 per cent of King's College Chapel, 37 per cent of St Alban's Cathedral, and 36 per cent of Tewkesbury Abbey. The Treasurer of Westminster Abbey reports that 'visitors provide more than two-thirds of what we need to run the Abbey' – over £800,000 in 1978 – 'and have enabled us to recoup heavy losses of over £100,000'. Bath Abbey, Salisbury Cathedral, and Winchester Cathedral all report that revenue from visitors is obviating the need for appeals for fabric repair. As a Bath spokesman says, 'we would rather the people who come and visit the Abbey should help pay for repairs than appeal from time to time to the public at large'. At Salisbury all the visitor revenue goes towards the continuous repair work, and more money from other sources has thereby been released to increase clergy stipends. At Wells, the accountant declares that 'we have an absolutely essential dependence on tourists, as we could not maintain the Cathedral and its services without their financial assistance'. Coventry Cathedral provides an example of a direct link between religious work and visitors' revenue, on which the cathedral's external ministries depend. The potential for increasing revenue from tourism seems considerable, particularly if admission charges were to be introduced at peak periods.

The boom in tourism also offers the cathedrals more than simply a financial opportunity. In the words of the Dean of Winchester, 'the Dean and Chapter try to make as much of the Cathedral available to the public as possible in the hope that its spiritual values will "rub off" on the visitors. Pains are taken to see that the services are as good as possible and that the vergers, musicians etc., are a credit to the Cathedral. Great importance is attached to the work of the Holiday Chaplains. We want to treat visitors as human beings and not as tourists to be exploited!' And the Archdeacon of Rochester is 'quite convinced that the Cathedral is a major place for evangelism and that we should make it available to as many people as possible – preferably with a guide so that the living side of the Cathedral can be underlined as well as the historic and architectural'.

Visiting a cathedral is not a casual experience for most visitors. Nearly three quarters of those ETB surveyed at eleven cathedrals during August 1978 said that they 'particularly wanted to see this cathedral' or 'a' cathedral. Many had come long distances; to visit York and Coventry cathedrals more than 40 per cent of their visitors had travelled more than fifty miles. At five of the cathedrals surveyed a quarter or more of visitors claimed to spend over an hour inside the cathedral: the proportion reached 37 per cent in Canterbury and 40 per cent in Durham.

The economic importance of cathedral tourism is indicated by the expenditure of at least £5 million yearly at Canterbury, of which about £1½ million is retained as net income by local hoteliers, shopkeepers, etc. The high proportion of foreigners amongst such visitors suggests that cathedrals are significant earners of foreign exchange.

To summarize, whilst tourism is becoming an increasingly helpful source of revenue for cathedral maintenance and repair, it must be managed so that the religious atmosphere and activities of cathedrals are not spoiled either by the tourists themselves or by over-commercialization of the cathedrals. In the words of the Dean of Ripon, cathedrals must 'give complete priority to the sense of worship, beauty, order, space – people come because they are hungry for beauty, mystery, and dignity. We must not allow clutter or money-making to cheat them of what they need.'

FURTHER READING

Alderson, William T., and Low, Shirley P. *The Interpretation of Historic Sites*. Nashville, Tennessee: American Association for State and Local History, 1976. Considers the practical problems of developing and conducting interpretation programmes for historic sites. Covers presenting the site, methods of interpretation, interpretation for school tours, selection and training of interpreters, and security.

Beazley, Elisabeth. *The Countryside on View*. London: Constable, 1971; paperback, Swansea: Christopher Davies, 1975. Handbook on display techniques of countryside centres, field museums, and historic buildings open to the public.

Binney, Marcus, and Burman, Peter. *Chapels & Churches: Who Cares. An Independent Report*. London: British Tourist Authority/Country Life, 1977. An exhaustive study of the material problems facing British churches of all Christian denominations: their care, raising money for repairs, closure, abandonment, vandalism, demolition, adaptation, and new uses.

Binney, Marcus, and Hanna, Max. *Preservation Pays: Tourism and the Economic Benefits of Conserving Historic Buildings*. London: SAVE Britain's Heritage [1978]. Deals with historic towns, cathedral cities, villages, ancient monuments, country houses, churches, gardens, etc.

191

The Future of our Heritage

English Cathedrals and Tourism: Problems and Opportunities. London: English Tourist Board, 1979. An analysis of the impact of tourism on English cathedrals, covering visitor patterns, revenue and costs, visitor management problems and practices, interpretation, publicity and liaison, and management structures.

English Heritage Monitor. English Tourist Board, yearly since 1977. Statistical analysis, with thirty-page commentary, of trends affecting England's architectural heritage. Deals with visitor trends and presentation to the public as well as conservation.

CHAPTER 12

Popularity: its Benefits and Risks

ELISABETH BEAZLEY

THE CONCERN of this chapter is the popularity of 'places of heritage' in the United Kingdom; conditions overseas can be very different. Here the pattern of towns and the countryside which we most cherish tends to be small both in size and in scale. We also have a large mobile population which is increasingly being encouraged to visit such places. Many of us are now horrified by the overwhelming numbers who come to some of our monuments, historic houses and those parts of the country known as beauty spots. At the same time yet more visitors are encouraged.

Why this contradiction? Gate money might be the quick answer but it is one that needs scrutiny. Can we afford to encourage visitors? Can we afford to keep them away?

In many cases the very survival of a 'place of heritage' may now depend on tourism. Marcus Binney and Max Hanna point out in *Preservation Pays* (1978) that 'Britain's historic buildings, quite apart from their intrinsic value and beauty, are a major economic resource and an irreplaceable capital asset, contributing significantly through tourism to earnings of foreign exchange, to local employment and prosperity, and to central government taxation'. The same might well be said of Britain's landscape, agricultural, woodland, or wild.

Economics lie at the root of that common misconception which has made the popularity of a place the yardstick against which to gauge its success. How else can success be measured? But from the point of view of the survival of the place itself and of the experience of those who come to visit it, popularity may spell disaster.

Conservation of atmosphere is clearly as important as that of fabric. Popularity militates against both; it is indeed a mixed blessing. Places once intended for enjoyment of a few for part of the time are now all too often expected to absorb large crowds most of the time. This is as true of big spaces as of small. The Epping Forest Centenary Appeal of 1978 says: 'The tide of traffic brings people in such numbers all the year round as to put at risk the very place

It is as essential not to wreck tranquillity as it is to prevent carpets becoming threadbare or grass becoming brown mud. There is a grave danger of killing the goose that lays the golden egg. Worse, we kill the thing we most treasure. Success in terms of visitor numbers can do this with shattering ease; yet gate-money is thought to be vital to survival. to survival.

It is our job as conservationists to recognize the ingredients of this dilemma and our job as planners to get the mix right.

The first assumption which must be challenged is that a visit to 'a place of heritage', be it a stately home, cathedral, castle, garden or lonely mountain or stretch of coast is an experience that all right-minded people enjoy or should be encouraged to enjoy. Because we greatly enjoy such things ourselves, we tend to imagine that others would share our enthusiasms given the chance. (There is a similarity here to that other cherished English belief: nice people like cricket, dogs and gardening. Though many do, others, equally charming, civilized and intelligent, do not.)

So we set out to attract more and more visitors, often as much in a spirit of evangelism as for financial gain. Our anxiety to increase the general interest can result in an urge to make everything accessible both physically and in terms of information. This includes the didactic attempt to 'interpret' everything, to 'bring out its meaning' for the good of others (and, perhaps, often because 'interpretation' itself is such an enjoyable exercise). Then everything tends to be 'on show', nothing is left to speak for itself or to chance discovery; the whole country becomes an exhibition.

Visitor numbers may rise, though probably not spectacularly; atmosphere, however, is irrevocably eroded.

This is not to decry all interpretation. That would be absurd: it is necessary only to look around to see the excellent work that has been done (from a parish church to the Ironbridge Gorge Museum). But quality in siting and type of medium (guide, guidebook, exhibition) are all important. It is 'unjustified to turn a wilderness into a circus for the sake of the doubtful benefit of education or of entertainment', points out Colin Tubbs in the Society for the Interpretation of Britain's Heritage *News Letter* (Autumn 1976). The same might be said of buildings or gardens. We are also warned against 'platitudes, misleading generalisations and an avoidance of real issues. Often the interpreter was talking to the converted and the spoon-feeding of the public could create a generation who found the countryside only on a nature trail.' Or a garden, on a horticultural walk.

Have we, the visitors, changed during the last thirty years? Yes, it seems we have. Around 1950, most of those visiting a country house did so because of their interest in country houses, just as the majority of those now attending, say, a golf tournament or a motor race are there because of their interest in golf or racing cars. Now perhaps 80 per cent of those visiting a country house on a sunny Sunday are doing so for the fun of a day out.

Why not? A parallel instance is the not unusual practice of sitting in the car in the country to read the Sunday paper. This is an eminently sensible place to enjoy the newspaper if you happen to be blessed with a comfortable motor-car but lack a comfortable fireside or a sunny garden. It too is part of the day out. In the same sort of way to the family visiting the country house, tea matters. It always has done. But sheer numbers mean a tea-shop rather than cucumber sandwiches on the lawn with the owner (and, of course, an unparalleled parking problem).

Several millions of us want and need this day out in the country – whence the introduction of Country Parks under the Countryside Act. However, we, the public, quite naturally confuse the use we make of the place we visit. No clear-cut decision is taken as to *whether we go there to enjoy ourselves in pleasant surroundings or to enjoy the place itself.* Most of us want a bit of both; perhaps much less of the latter than may be generally suspected.

Part of the answer to the hideous dilemma of popularity lies in distinguishing between the sociable and the solitary places. There are still many fine stretches of coastline and remote valleys where half a dozen people make a crowd. Conversely, the summit of Snowdon can be really rather jolly with sightseers on every pinnacle, like a craggy race meeting (but even here we aggravate a conservation problem which dates back, perhaps, to the late eighteenth century).

Less generally recognized is the idea of segregating the sociable and solitary places within a site: not a new idea, but one which perhaps needs to be practised more in our small-scale country. Owners who have recognized the need for, and the fun of, the 'day out' have provided for it with great success, but this often seems to have been done with the sole intention of increasing the gate-money: there has been little attempt to use it as a planning tool to mitigate the erosion of either the fabric or the atmosphere. As a result, increasing numbers of visitors further undermine both their own enjoyment and the place they have come to enjoy.

The 'jewel' (house, garden, church, castle, cliff) should be considered in its broadest setting. Access to it should be limited so as to keep the numbers to a tolerable level. The siting of car parks is all-important in this respect. At the same time, there should be plenty of other things to do in addition to enjoying the focal point; these will also allow for timed tickets to the focal point. People may be happy to pay gate-money to return again and again without wishing to re-visit 'the main attraction', particularly in the case of houses set within big parks.

Careful analysis of what the place has to offer and a clear

distinction between its unique (and often vulnerable) foci and other parts which may be designed to offer the enjoyment of 'a day out' can go a long way towards a solution if the results of such an analysis are integrated in a plan to deflect pressure.

Indeed, there are places where it might be wiser to put capital into a money-making counter-attraction at some distance from the site, than to lure more visitors to hasten its destruction. If a monument, say, is felt to have 'enough' visitors, a car-park a mile or so away might offer a first-rate, scholarly-based interpretative centre, and perhaps a skateboard rink, a tree-top assault course, a swimming-pool or some such attraction. The distance would filter the 'day-outers' from the 'site-seers' to the advantage of both. For the former, a distant view of the monument, or even the knowledge of its existence, may be enough – such knowledge gives us all a sense of continuity and of security. During a discussion some years ago about national parks and wilderness areas, a member of the US Congress was challenged as to whether he had ever been to the place in question. He said he had not, but to *know that it was there* was what mattered to him.

So we must resist the temptation to encourage as many visitors as possible, willy-nilly; it is essential to be selective. Incidentally, a regular event, enjoyed locally and thus integrated with, although not actually staged at, the place in question, can both serve as a non-eroding fund-raiser and increase consciousness of that place. The church fête provides a traditional example.

The Dean and Chapter of Lincoln Cathedral have followed such an argument to its logical conclusion. A committee representing them runs a local motor-cycling race track meeting once a year, from which all profits are donated to the cathedral funds. The Dean and Chapter themselves own a motor-cycle which races under cathedral colours – but not, as yet, with the Dean in the saddle.

This chapter has dwelt much more on the risks of popularity than on its benefits because the benefits are evident. But they must not be forgotten, and they are not only financial. Some places are immensely enjoyable in the excitement of a crowd. A cathedral brimming with people who are not there primarily to sightsee (a medieval pilgrimage must have been tremendous fun, although hardly peaceful); a pipe-band drawing crowds to a great courtyard: Beating Retreat in a castle bailey; horsey events and regattas – all can transform a 'place of heritage' enjoyably – perhaps because we, as visitors, identify ourselves with our fellow spectators in seeing it as a backdrop to a spectacle. What few of us want are queues and crowds in what was intended to be a peaceful setting.

Planning for the beneficial reception of large numbers lies in care over many seemingly humble details. These include:

1. *Means of access and location of entrances*, in relation both to the public roads and to the site itself. A site cannot be opened until these problems are satisfactorily resolved with the Highway Authority.

2. *The siting of car and coach parks.* While minimizing visual intrusion, this is perhaps the most important single factor in any plan since it decides which parts are to be most crowded and most accessible within a site.

3. *Payment by visitors.* Where and for what? This is integral with visitor management. With (4) below it can allow for timed tickets to the focal point of the site.

4. *Provision and siting of alternative magnets* to the focal point, whether educational (an exhibition), energy-consuming (an adventure playground), or just a sunny, sheltered place to picnic not far from a car park.

5. *Extension of opening hours and seasons.* This does little to spread the visitor load at peak times, but it gives the more solitary-minded a chance. Such extensions must take into account that the fabric, particularly that of historic houses, needs a periodic rest, and that maintenance, including housework, must be carried on. We must also realize that it is at times necessary to 'shut the gate' from the point of view of both the visitor and the property, when the place is full enough.

6. *The visual results of capital grants.* Because capital is forthcoming

18 The sanitized past: Department of the Environment greensward at an English ancient monument

19 The past left to itself: Thomas Gray's churchyard, Stoke Poges, Buckinghamshire

for new projects but not for maintenance, things are often 'overdone' – e.g., macadamized surfaces of car parks when grass or chippings would answer. This reversal of traditional country-estate practice is insidiously transforming much of rural Britain.

7. *A moderation of the democratic urge*, which now operates to the detriment of both place and visitor. Not everybody can enjoy everything all the time. People should sometimes be able to pay more to enjoy a comparatively solitary visit, as for example on 'connoisseurs' days'. But such privileges must be limited lest they exclude those who cannot afford them. A system of advance booking, with a limited number of tickets available on the day, as practised by the Royal Society for the Protection of Birds, might be introduced for popular monuments and houses.

8. *Schools' and children's visits.* Much has been done in this respect (the National Trust's Youth Theatre is a fascinating, although expensive, example), but many youngsters' visits are still a disaster – so boring to the child as to put him off for life, and so disruptive to the general public as to stretch their affection for the young to breaking point. Education has a vital part to play in showing that such places can add imeasurably to the enjoyment of life. Site management should take advantage of the fact that schools' visits come at a different time of year from the main visitor onslaught.

9. *Encouragement of local interest in local places out of season.* We tend not to visit locally, but the cost of petrol could focus interest nearer home. Unemployment may also affect this in several ways (more time, less money).

10. *The use of the media*, particularly TV, to increase under-standing and enhance enjoyment. The media must be used with great discretion, however, for visitor numbers soar after almost any TV programme about a place; the popularity can be ruinous as well as lucrative.

11. *The provision of visitor services.* A well-designed and sited shop and a simple restaurant can greatly add to enjoyment and income. Such provision usually increases visitor numbers.

12. *Allowing the visitor to discover things for himself*, or appear to do so. But this, too, may need to be planned: e.g., the principal visitor route might be diverted to avoid a particularly attractive or 'secret' part of an estate.

13. *Allowing a place to remain itself.* Leave the unfashionable alone, and avoid gimmicks.

Each place is unique; that is its greatest asset. It seems to me that the gravest risk we run in managing 'places of heritage' is unconsciously ironing out their differences in a misguided attempt to help the visitor. The same lettering on everyone's signs, however well designed; the same goods in the shops, however good the taste; the same picnic table.... Uniqueness is also undermined by too much well-meant information. The stimulation of exploring the unknown is foregone if the visitor is deprived of all sense of bewilderment and wonder, or the possibility of losing himself even temporarily.

FURTHER READING

Aldridge, Don. *Guide to Countryside Interpretation, Part One: Principles of Countryside Interpretation and Interpretive Planning.* Edinburgh: HMSO, for Countryside Commission, 1975. The philosophy and underlying principles of interpretation by the Director of Conservation Education for the Countryside Commission for Scotland.

Beazley, Elisabeth. *The Countryside on View: A Handbook on Countryside Centres, Field Museums, and Historic Buildings Open to the Public.* London: Constable, 1971; paperback, Swansea: Christopher Davies, 1975. A small reference book. The nuts and bolts of the principles underlying display and protection aimed at containing the visual impact of popularity.

Binney, Marcus, and Hanna, Max. *Preservation Pays: Tourism and the Economic Benefits of Conserving Historic Buildings.* London: SAVE Britain's Heritage [1978]. Patterns of tourism and its impact in cities, villages and the open countryside in the context of the title. All kinds of buildings and monuments are considered.

Interpretation. Newsletter of the Society for the Interpretation of Britain's Heritage. Manchester Polytechnic, Centre for Environmental Interpretation. In existence since 1975, this Society aims 'to promote a high standard of interpretation in order to heighten public awareness and appreciation of Britain's heritage'.

Montagu, Lord, of Beaulieu. *The Gilt and the Gingerbread, or How to Live in a Stately Home and Make Money.* London: Michael Joseph, 1967. Witty and still relevant account of the author's success in making Beaulieu one of Britain's best-known and best-paying historic sites, with chapters on maintenance and upkeep, catering and souvenirs, publicity and promotion, etc.

Parks: An International Journal for Managers of National Parks, Historic Sites, and Other Protected Areas. Washington, D.C.: International Union for the Conservation of Nature and Natural Resources.

Quarterly, since 1976. Worldwide coverage of problems of heritage management and interpretation.

Pennyfather, Keith. *Guide to Countryside Interpretation, Part Two: Interpretive Media and Facilities.* Edinburgh: HMSO for Countryside Commission, 1975. In addition to sections outlined in the title, appendices with useful addresses and a long bibliography are included.

Tilden, Freeman. *Interpreting our Heritage: Principles and Practices for Visitor Services in Parks, Museums, and Historic Places.* Chapel Hill: University of North Carolina Press, 1957. Still the standard account of the basic principles of interpretation, in the United States, with a chapter dealing specifically with historic sites.

CHAPTER 13

Oppression to Obsession

MARCUS BINNEY

'YOU SHOULD always try to turn a disadvantage to your own advantage', a pre-budget *Sunday Telegraph* article (8 March 1981) by Ivan Fallon suggested to the Chancellor of the Exchequer: 'I know a number of highly successful businessmen who employ it as their first principle.' So I often think it is with historic buildings. Some have only to look at them for their minds to be filled with a picture of endlessly escalating maintenance costs, huge heating bills and constant repairs. Yet for others every empty or decaying old building is an opportunity to acquire or adapt something of real character, to give it a new lease of life.

Historic buildings, like businesses, often demand an entrepreneurial approach. Those who see them principally as a burden are of two types. One is the speculator, the developer who wishes to be rid of them for financial gain. The other is the administrator, who grudges the time and money absorbed in looking after older buildings or lacks the expertise, advice or imagination to see how they could be adapted in a practical and economical way. Both types are often obsessed by the idea that a new building replacing the old one will somehow be magically maintenance-free.

Owners who protest that their historic buildings are white elephants often have never attempted the most obvious economic test — offering them for sale on reasonable terms on the open market. One council in north-east England, wishing to demolish its former town hall, had never offered it for sale, and when challenged merely postulated that everyone knew it was available anyway. Yet if a building is not advertised, if no price or conditions are set, the chances of potential purchasers coming forward are minimal.

Mr Michael Heseltine, Secretary of State for the Environment, has spoken out against such anti-preservation behaviour. Authorities and owners, he stated at Chester on 14 March 1980, are 'to explore every possible way of keeping the building, and that may include offering the building for sale — usually freehold — on the open market with flexible uses and an openness of mind to any reasonable opportunity that emerges'.

In the United States, the Federal Government has turned the tables on Federal agencies seeking to demolish buildings on the National Register of Historic Places. Section 106 of the National Historic Preservation Act of 1966 states that before demolition can proceed, the agency must undertake elaborate feasibility studies to explore how the property might be saved and adapted. This reverses the traditional ploy whereby a government department merely commissions expert advisers who produce alarming figures about costs of repair, and problems of adapting, letting, or finding tenants.

One block that preservationists in Britain repeatedly face is the belief, dating from the 1950s and 1960s but still fixed in the minds of many senior officials and managers, that modern architecture aided by science and technology can in a matter of decades provide mankind with a wholly satisfactory new environment. Yet in all these blueprints for cities of the future no attempt was made to estimate the cost, let alone to consider where the finance would come from. It was simply, confidently assumed that continuing economic expansion would provide the necessary resources. This attitude was not confined to architecture and the building industry, but ran through all spheres of business activity and planning. 'My generation (40-ish),' William Keegan wrote in the *Observer* (February 1981), 'was led to believe that by the time we got to where we are ... everything would be under control, economic policy would be brilliantly planned, and such problems as there might be would be the problems of plenty.'

Another block that the preservation movement faces is a built-in resistance among many decision-makers to the idea of preserving historic buildings. As one official in the Property Service Agency said to us apropos the SAVE report on goverment offices and town halls ('Glittering Palaces for Bureaucrats', *Building Design*, 11 November 1977, pp. 25-48), 'Of course I'm all in favour of conservation — I'm a member of the National Trust, but some of these people, they want to preserve everything.' When one asks for instances where conservation has gone too far, it is often hard to get an answer.

Max Hanna and my *Preservation Pays* (1978) at last persuaded one government official holding a number of purse-strings that historic houses and sites, far from being a permanent drain on public funds, contributed through tourism to employment, tax receipts and prosperity. However, he immediately thought of a new argument against preservation: 'the image of history and Beefeaters was making it difficult for British exporters to sell our goods abroad'; historic buildings as much as a reputation for strikes were bringing Britain down. But he produced no evidence to substantiate this view, just a deeply-rooted suspicion that historic buildings are a burden.

This idea that the past is a burden, a straight-jacket in the way of progress, constantly recurs. It can be traced back to a considerable extent, I think, to Ruskin's much-quoted views on preservation in *Seven Lamps of Architecture* (1849):

It is . . . no question of expediency or feeling whether we shall preserve the buildings of past times or not. *We have no right whatever to touch them.* They are not ours. They belong partly to those who built them, and partly to all the generations of mankind who are to follow us. The dead have still their right in them.

Ruskin's cry of hands-off was not only understandable but absolutely essential in view of the over-zealous church restoration of his time. But Ruskin's concern was principally for the medieval buildings which were his enduring passion.

And though his strictures against preservation and his exhortations to leave well alone deserve equally to be applied to outstanding buildings of later periods, for example to great country houses which retain their contents and their setting intact, they were not, I think, aimed at the much wider range of buildings we now seek to retain and to put to constructive use. Ruskin's feelings were aroused by buildings which today would be classed as monuments. Yet the spectre that historic buildings are a crippling burden imposed on society by preservationists survives. By the end of this century, suggested the Minister responsible for conservation in a speech at Leicester University in 1978, 'conservation would be in competition with the National Health Service and other services. We have to be very sure,' she added, 'that society as a whole understands this and accepts it, and is prepared to devote a very substantial element of national resources to supporting old buildings.' This was at a time when the National Health Service was costing £6 billion a year, whereas grants to historic buildings, to which she was referring, were £7.7 million — one-ninth of one per cent of the cost of the Health Service.

It is another fallacy to say that towns and cities must choose between a modern architecture suited to our own needs and aspirations and the straitjacket of the past. Many older buildings can be excellently, indeed inspiringly, adapted to contemporary needs and demands.

The choice we have to make is not in fact between old and new, but between a genuine past and a contrived past. In a splendid paper delivered to the 1978 Victorian Society Conference, Roderick Gradidge argued that the true main stream of twentieth-century architecture was not the modern movement or the so-called International style, but neo-Tudor, running from the Arts and Crafts Movement through the suburbs of the 1920s to the pubs of Roy Wilson Smith. The huge Arndale Centre at Manchester, for example, was widely heralded in the 1970s as bringing the latest in transatlantic shopping developments to a nineteenth-century industrial town. Yet look a little closer and what does one find in the middle of a sea of concrete: a new olde-worlde pub built to the scale of a traditional street. The same phenomenon can be seen in France. Brand-new chalet-style auberges are fitted out in pseudo-Troubadour style – an upmarket version of Merrie England.

If we leave ourselves without a genuine past, a past will have to be invented. All over the island of Corfu in the autumn of 1978, for example, were signs saying, 'If you haven't been to the Village, you haven't seen Corfu'. The Village was supposed to give visitors an experience of the life and character of a traditional Corfu village. In fact it is a wholly artificial creation. The entrance is marked by a huge screen wall worthy of an imposing country club, with parking for a fleet of motor coaches. Once past the ticket booth you find the village pond, carefully moulded in concrete. The buildings attempt to look vernacular, with plaster chipped away under each arch to a regular pattern to create a sense of age and gentle decay.

Some may think the current obsession for reproducing past styles is a transient phenomenon, that 'heritage' kitchens with country woodwork will pass out of fashion as inevitably as their formica predecessors. In this view the past is currently being used as a form of wallpaper. But taste for reproduction in fact derives from the more general need for material evidence of the past. Reflecting on the sudden increase of appreciation of industrial buildings, such as power stations, Glyn England, Chairman of the Central Electricity Generating Board (press release, 17 February 1981), wondered why it is that

buildings associated with initially unwelcome developments have become accepted, and even revered, sometimes within the span of a single generation. And why should this revaluation of controversial aspects of the past, this affection for the symbols of earlier and unpopular progress, be especially characteristic of our own time? I am not sure it can be wholly explained in terms of a growing awareness of the architectural merits or historical associations of the buildings concerned. Its roots may lie deeper.

20 Historical pastiche at King's Dominion near Richmond, Virginia

21 A reproduction in old vernacular style at the 'Village', Corfu

22 Modern 'Gothic': Belvedere Hotel, Melbourne, Australia

23 Old-time rural nostalgia under a modern shopping centre: Johannes-
burg, South Africa

We are living in an acutely uncertain age. At the same time, because of rapidly advancing technology and social and other trends, we are experiencing perpetual change in almost every aspect of our daily lives.

While much of this change is necessary, it could nevertheless be argued that people's capacity to absorb it, particularly in an age of international uncertainty and tension, is becoming strained. Does their regard for old buildings therefore denote, in part, not simply nostalgia but a rational hunger for some degree of permanence? Are they, consiously or instinctively, seeking reassurance from solid, everyday, familiar things?

Only the passage of time can answer the questions Mr England raises. Some think that when more confident and prosperous times arrive, people may swing away from preservation in favour of large-scale redevelopment of a radical kind. The current concern for conserving and recycling historic buildings, I believe, may mark a true Rubicon. The Montagu Committee report, *Britain's Historic Buildings: A Policy for their Future Use* (1980, p. 4), saw 'the current concern for conservation' not just as one extreme of a pendulum swing but 'as one of those fundamental shifts or watersheds in man's attitude towards the world in which he lives. . . . Espousal of a particular period or style no longer automatically brings in train a rejection of that which preceded or followed it.'

It is sometimes charged, particularly by architects, that we are the first generation without confidence in the architecture of our own age. On the contrary, the post-war era is the first to abandon confidence not just in the styles of previous ages, but in almost its entire building legacy. Many medieval buildings were destroyed as a result of Renaissance and subsequent classical preferences, but no previous age has ever indulged in such wholesale condemnation of the architecture of the past. The idea that conservation is an obstacle to progress was forcefully challenged by Mrs Jennifer Jenkins, Chairman of the Historic Buildings Council for England, at a seminar on the Montagu Report held by the British Tourist Authority at

Oppression to Obsession

the Royal Society of Arts on 19 March 1981:

I doubt if conservation is the enemy of urban revival; rather it is the agent. If we want people to return to the inner city we have to induce them to work and live there. Those towns which have kept their older buildings and have designated conservation areas are benefitting economically. The alternative in many cases is not new development but simply more vacant sites.

The need now is to establish coexistence between past and present creations. As Randolph Langenbach asked in *A Future from the Past* (1977, p. 115), 'Is it not better to *add* to the sum total of the record of human creativity than to subtract from it?' Are there not enough opportunities for new buildings without destroying fine or worthwhile buildings from the past?

FURTHER READING

Adaptive Use: Development Economics, Process and Profiles. Washington, D.C.: Urban Land Institute, 1978. Studies on planning, financing, and programming projects of re-use.

Binney, Marcus, and Hanna, Max. *Preservation Pays: Tourism and the Economic Benefits of Conserving Historic Buildings.* London: SAVE Britain's Heritage [1978]. Assessment of benefits which accrue as a result of tourism both in terms of foreign exchange and of taxation to the national exchequer.

Diamonstein, Barbaralee. *Buildings Reborn: New Uses, Old Places.* New York: Harper & Row, 1978. Case studies of a wide range of building types put to different uses.

Harvey, John H. *Conservation of Buildings.* London: John Baker, 1972. Classic study of the growth of the preservation movement with a wide-ranging discussion of the issues involved.

Kidney, Walter C. *Working Places: The Adaptive Use of Industrial Buildings.* Pittsburgh: Ober Park Associates, 1976. Contains a series of excellent case studies with details of construction and cost.

Langenbach, Randolph. *A Future from the Past: The Case for Conservation and Reuse of Old Buildings in Industrial Communities.* Washington, D.C.: US Department of Housing and Urban Development and the Massachusetts Department of Community Affairs, 1977. Case studies, discussions of costs and benefits, and constructive proposals for conservation policy.

McNulty, Robert H., and Kliment, Stephen A. *Neighborhood Conservation: A Handbook on Methods and Techniques.* New York: The Whitney Library of Design, 1976. Handbook of numerous methods and techniques suggesting what local communities can do in America, in terms of conserving buildings and reviving community life.

Massachusetts, Department of Community Affairs. *Built to Last: A Handbook on Recycling Old Buildings.* Washington, D.C.: The Preservation Press, 1977. Series of case studies by building type.

Montagu, Lord, of Beaulieu. *Britain's Historic Buildings: A Policy for Their Future Use.* London: British Tourist Authority [1980]. Based on extensive consultation and documentation. Discusses the principal building types at risk and the roles and responsibilities of private and public sectors, and presents a series of recommendations for the conservation and re-use of older buildings.

Warner, Raynor M., Groff, Sibyl McCormac, and Warner, Ranne P., with Weiss, Sandi. *Business and Preservation.* New York: Inform, 1978; also retitled *New Profits from Old Buildings: Private Enterprise Approaches to Making Preservation Pay.* New York: McGraw Hill, 1978. Case studies of buildings which have been adapted, with useful financial and technical details.

Conclusion: Dilemmas of Preservation

DAVID LOWENTHAL

EVERY ASPECT of our heritage seems more dramatically altered and drastically threatened today than ever before. To cite just one instance, more of prehistory is said to have been destroyed in the past generation than was previously known to exist. 'The tempo of destruction is currently so great', warns Karl Meyer in *The Plundered Past* (1974, p. xv), 'that by the end of the century most important archaeological sites may well be plundered or paved over. We face a future in which there may be no past beyond that which is already known and excavated or . . . what is left may be so ruinously mutilated as to afford only a forlorn fragment of a vanished legacy.' No less than archaeological sites, historic buildings and traditional landscapes are victims of modern technology.

Such destruction is not uniquely modern, to be sure. Thomas Bateman's *Vestiges of the Antiquities of Derbyshire* (1848, p. 286) noted the 'rapid disappearance and exhaustion' of ancient monuments owing to 'agricultural improvements, and the ill conducted pillage of idle curiosity'. Public interest threatened the survival of British ancient monuments as much as a century ago, according to a contributor to the *Edinburgh Review* (1881, pp. 120-1): 'The very fact that attention is drawn to them makes them increasingly the prey of the ignorant sightseer on the one hand or the needy owner of the soil on the other.'

Yet the pace of destruction has unquestionably accelerated in our own day. Giant machinery can now transform a city or a landscape almost in the twinkling of an eye; where damage might formerly have been halted before too much harm was done, today trees are felled, hedgerows uprooted, buildings wholly demolished before a protest can be lodged. Deep ploughing obliterates visual evidence

213

of settlement patterns that had survived two millennia of previous grazing and cultivation. Farmers, sand and gravel contractors, and developers make increasing inroads against surviving landscapes. Modern weapons annihilate terrain and vegetation as well as man-made structures. Industrial pollution erodes ancient masterpieces from the Acropolis to *The Last Supper*, which can perhaps now be salvaged only by depriving Athens and Milan of both automobiles and industry.

Technology is the past's major enemy, but other agencies add to the toll of destruction. Patriots who eradicate what they regard as relics of and monuments to a depraved or unhappy era are apt to uproot the entire heritage in their iconoclastic fervour. Zeal for knowledge may destroy the past in the course of studying it, as archaeological excavation still unhappily demonstrates. The most ancient living tree ever found – a bristlecone pine 4,900 years old – was cut down to determine its age. The crowned mummified head of Otokar II, king of Bohemia, rapidly disintegrated when his thirteenth-century tomb was re-opened in Prague's St. Vitus Cathedral. 'That's the trouble with old mysteries, they can't stand touching', commented the *International Herald Tribune* (25 January, 1977). 'For 700 years Otokar lay there in peace, while the Czechs wondered what had happened to him, and now he has gone.'

Mass tourism has intensified the impact of theft and erosion at historic sites. Visitors to Stratford no longer take home slivers of Anne Hathaway's supposed chair, nor do visitors to Salisbury Plain hire hammers at Amesbury to chip keepsakes from Stonehenge. But these improvements in decorum are minor compared with modern losses. The press of visitors destroyed the turf around the sarsens at Stonehenge. Human breath promoted micro-organic decay that forced the closure of the cave paintings at Lascaux. Sightseers at Canterbury and other cathedrals, Max Hanna's chapter tells us, wear down old floors, render inscriptions illegible, and pilfer fittings. High prices for antiquities have promoted illicit trade and devastated ancient sites; entire

Mayan temples in Central America are broken up for clandestine export.

But protecting historic sites and artifacts may equally doom them beyond recognition. Modern fire and safety regulations in adapted historic buildings in Britain, for example, require insulation and escape routes so expensive or unsightly that strict adherence to them would jeopardize the survival of most Georgian and Victorian domestic architecture.

Outright destruction is not the only force that profoundly alters our surroundings; so does the decay of artifacts of all kinds – houses, clothes, books, toys, furniture, crockery. Far more plentiful than ever before, such things also expire at a pace our ancestors never witnessed. When raw materials were expensive and labour comparatively cheap, objects of use were made to last. Household artifacts were often passed on to the next generation. Today, by contrast, we replace rather than conserve and repair. Who now protects fabrics with dust covers? How many of us turn cuffs and collars or darn socks? Manufacturing makes it cheaper to replace aggregates than to fit new parts into old structures; and as profits depend on continuing sales, fashion persuades us that still serviceable older possessions are obsolete.

Thus we live in circumstances previous generations would have found extraordinary: most of the things we wear, use, and see around us are shorter-lived than ourselves. At the same time, our own longevity has increased. And we have become increasingly mobile, with fewer and fewer of us living in the places, let alone the same houses, in which we were born. Hence the environments and artifacts that surround us in later life are now seldom those we grew up with. Ever more disposable, the things we make and build are also more and more apt to be left behind.

The modern impulse toward preservation is partly a reaction to the increasing evanescence of the things that pass through our lives. We cling all the more to the little that remains familiar. And we compensate for a less well known environment with a heightened interest in its

215

history. Like a newcomer to an old village who self-consciously acquires roots by joining the local historical society, the annual buyer of new clothes and cars becomes nostalgically attached to the articles he discards. After they cease to be useful they are admired because they are old. Such collectibles are precious because they give the objects we once used a genealogy, place them in a temporal context, make up for the longevity we deprived them of by having cast them off so soon. Interest in each aspect of the heritage mounts as it threatens to disappear – steam engines, parish churches, thatched roofs, canals, pottery ovens all mirror an affection for the vanishing past they seldom elicited when still plentiful.

The pace of change increases attachments to scenes recalled from childhood, things that were here before us. Links with the past mitigate the strangeness of ever less familiar surroundings. Dissatisfaction with the present and malaise about the future induce many to look back with nostalgia, to equate what is beautiful and livable with what is old or past. The sense of place and the significance of community promote the endurance of landmarks and landscapes in locales as disparate as Leeds and Dartmoor, as Ken Powell's and Sylvia Sayer's chapters show. And the diffusion of history and archaeology makes us aware that scenes of our past are essential ingredients of our present identity – a country without historic buildings is like a man without a memory.

Tastes for the past have changed no less than the past itself, as Michael Hunter and Hugh Prince here remind us. Greek, Roman, and various stages of Gothic and countless other traditions have attracted admiration and emulation in differing epochs. Today's concern embraces all past periods, and to earlier aesthetic, scientific, pedagogic, and patriotic reasons for conservation, our generation adds social identity, a growing need for roots and traditions, and the saving of resources.

Appalled by the destruction of the past, we apply greater care and expertise to the preservation of what survives.

The technological tools that advance demolition also locate history hitherto hidden from view under the ground, beneath the sea, behind the varnish of a painting. New conservation techniques now mend old materials, fabrics, structures that used to decay beyond hope of repair. To maintain a cathedral is not yet cheap or easy, but scientific renovation is now both less obtrusive and more durable than ever before.

The surviving past looms more prominently also because more and more around us is recognized as old and hence thought worthwhile. Antiques once had to date from another century, but today include items from the 1950s; buildings thought worth saving in Britain, once exclusively pre-Georgian, now stem from epochs as recent as the 1930s; in the United States anything older than fifty years qualifies for historic preservation grants; yesterday's ephemera, once simply junk, are now collectibles with documented lineages; nostalgia, formerly reserved for childhood if not for remote antiquity, now lends last year a golden glow. The officially valued French past now extends from palaeolithic Lascaux to Le Corbusier. In Britain, the Department of the Environment has doubled the number of listed buildings in a decade, as much by adding Victorian structures to the earlier list as by discovering previously overlooked older ones.

Not even this expanded and better protected past satisfies the modern need for historical artifacts, buildings, and landscapes. The novelist Saki once said that 'the people of Crete make more history than they can consume locally'. That is a rare circumstance; in most countries the demand for history far exceeds the supply. Spurious originals bolster national pride, antiquing has become a widespread pursuit, newly-minted historic villages replicate fond images of the past. Seeing a quaint Mediterranean town, an inquiring visitor is told, 'the town *has* no history, ...it was built from scratch three years ago entirely for the tourist trade'.

The more the past is destroyed or left behind, the more

pervasive grows our nostalgia, the more obsessed we become with preservation and reconstruction. 'The dual impulse of our age,' suggests a conservationist in David Ely's novel *Time Out* (1968, p. 101), 'is vast devastation coupled with equally vast reconstruction.' In fact as well as fiction, preservation can sometimes be achieved only in the context of destruction. At Pompeii instantaneous catastrophe made possible total preservation; the subsequent recovery of the ordinary things of life – hairpins and ink pots, dice and knucklebones, mirrors and bottles – which no one would otherwise have bothered to save, lends our view of that ancient city a rare immediacy.

The dissolution of England's monasteries in the 1530s is another case in point; the king who had destroyed them championed Leland's studies of their literary remains, and their physical ruins were soon venerated as historical monuments. Ada Louise Huxtable recounts in *Kicked a Building Lately?* (1978) how an insurance company 'compensated' for demolishing Nashville's Grand Ole Opry House, by using the old bricks and artifacts for a 'Little Church of Opryland' in a new amusement park.

Thus the tangible past, increasingly threatened by technology, pollution, greed, neglect, and popularity, has become a battleground of conflicting interests. Survivals from earlier times today occupy our attention as never before.

This book is concerned no less with these threats to our heritage than with the problems we face when we translate our concern into action. The twin impulses of destruction and preservation engender four major dilemmas explored in this book: what to save from the past and why; how to use what we save; how to prevent the fake past from inundating the real; and how preservation, laudable in itself, can foster rather than hinder alternative uses of the past.

What should we save and why?

The criteria that mark buildings, artifacts and landscapes

24 New infill architecture behind old and restored buildings: Lafayette Square, Washington, DC

25 An old façade 'decorates' an out-sized building: ZCMI Center, Salt Lake City, Utah, c. 1975

for study and preservation are in constant flux. Structures unworthy of attention ten years ago have since acquired devotees; architects once forgotten gain new favour; works formerly thought derivative or trivial acquire value. Every passing generation tends to downgrade the deeds of its immediate forebears, while rehabilitating the reputation of a more remote past.

Features considered to be historically significant likewise change over time. Not only do particular figures and events gain fresh stature or fall into disrepute, but entire aspects of the past become newly worth saving or ripe for discarding. The homes of presidents and patriots, the sites of national battles and the routes of explorers used to be the most important American monuments; today's preservation priorities are linked with industry and the arts and with ethnic minorities. The antebellum plantation house now gives way as a focus of attention to slave quarters once hidden as shameful, just as workaday servants' wings at National Trust houses now attract British visitors whose predecessors had eyes only for the sumptuous and the aristocratic.

Attention has also shifted from things and places of high architectural merit or unique historical consequence to those that have played a part in the lives of ordinary people. The distinction bears on what the geographer Yi-Fu Tuan has called public symbols and fields of care ('Space and Place', 1974, pp. 237-43). Public symbols are widely venerated monuments – the Eiffel Tower, Big Ben, Niagara Falls. Fields of care are neighbourhoods whose features matter only to those intimately associated with them, everyday scenes that provide people with a durable sense of place. As the architect Lionel Brett writes in *Parameters and Images* (1970, p. 143):

The locality where we belong and feel we are 'somebody', originally nothing more than a big plane tree or a bench in the sun for the men, and the village pump for the women,... is a centre of reassurance.... We can identify it in an unfamiliar country more by the tenacity of its users than by its architecture,

26 The elite past preserved: Fairvue, the Isaac Franklin plantation house, Gallatin, Tennessee

27 The folk past preserved: restored slave quarters at Fairvue

it may even be ugly, will generally be shabby, will invariably be overcrowded.... Civic societies passionately defend its every cobblestone, but they defend more than brick and mortar, it is the need for what Simone Weil called *enracinement*, rootedness.

Historic preservation in this spirit extends to the industrial past, not just to factory buildings but to entire working-class towns. 'Our identity lies in this urban industrial past', as Jane Holtz Kay quotes Patrick Mogan, originator of America's first urban historic park, Lowell, Massachusetts. The Lowell revival involves a sense of '*collective* heritage' for those who lived there, a 'confirmation of their past' (*Nation*, 17 September, 1977).

Britain's industrial heritage has been markedly neglected despite – or perhaps because of – her primary role in the Industrial Revolution. Indeed, recent Pennine redevelopment fuelled a desire to *banish* old industrial images; civic leaders who viewed old mills and tenements with disgust and embarrassment felt that progress depended on erasing what was left of the nineteenth century. But responses to the 'Satanic Mills' exhibition recently staged by the Royal Institute of British Architects shows how much these structures meant to the people who lived and worked in them, even when they found life hard and the buildings ugly. Tamara Hareven and Randolph Langenbach here cite the visitor who was glad to see that her mill was still there – not wanting to go back to the days of toil as an eleven-year-old after a breakfast of bread and dripping, but feeling that the building's survival provided a physical continuity to match her memory.

The need for familiar landmarks, for being physically in touch with reminders of one's past, now animates many communities to save vernacular structures and humble scenes that would never qualify as outstandingly 'aesthetic' or 'historical'. 'The problem for planners and preservationists,' as Hareven and Langenbach say, 'is how to weld together in the preservation effort the two aspects of human association, the intimate, and that based on knowledge of art and history.' And Marion Shoard's essay notes that 'landscape features, particularly those which lie near our homes, form part of our collective identity. We are, in part, the places that have shaped our lives. If England's landscape is impoverished, so are our personalities.'

How should we use what we save?

No problem discussed in this book arouses greater concern among conservationists. The long-term survival of any structure clearly implies a use different from the original one. As things age they become ever less suited to their initial purposes, purposes which time may likewise extinguish or transform. Social and technological change have made the sacrificial altar, the village stocks, the clipper ship wholly obsolete. Many an old jail cannot serve as a prison today, nor can an early zoo be modernized, because ideas about how to treat captive animals and people have changed. Few if any unaltered old houses match modern standards of privacy and sanitation. Any contemporary use requires some adaptation to current notions of comfort, of social interaction, of technology, of safety, even of decor – adaptations which inevitably violate the historical integrity of what is inherited. Modern alterations that enable a structure to remain occupied and alive are bound to conflict with the yearning to retain familiar street scenes, landmarks, and other mementoes.

Adaptive re-use evokes passionate but quite disparate responses. North Americans take pride in the range of functions places have served: Lafayette Square in Washington, for example, for having been in turn a cherry orchard, the site of Andrew Jackson's raucous inaugural party, a sheep pasture during the First World War. The British, by contrast, have felt new use a sacrilege to old structures; hence Lord Anglesey's plea to the Friends of Friendless Churches that redundant churches be left vacant as perpetual reminders of spiritual and eternal values. Indeed, exemption from local taxes enjoyed by many listed buildings, if vacant, makes less likely their occupance by new users. Only things kept for use strictly as museum exhibits can remain faithful to historical structure and appearance.

But both conversion and museumization inevitably revise the past. Complete preservation means withdrawal from life; it embalms or pickles what is saved. Thoroughgoing re-use invalidates or trivializes surviving elements of the past. Public funding and tax benefits have made historic preservation attractive to American realtors, but the old 'Home Improvement Company', though now renamed 'Preservation Specialists', is apt to 'restore' as it once 'renewed', with little historic understanding and a ruthless disregard for continuity.

Increasing demands for access to the surviving past conflict, moreover, both with private ownership and with the need to discover history for oneself. The greatest part of the English countryside heritage remains, as Shoard points out in her *Theft of the Countryside* (1980), virtually inaccessible to public view. Partly as a consequence, overuse of the most accessible sites makes them increasingly unattractive. The press of visitors at many historic houses and ancient monuments requires fences, guards, and other paraphernalia that erode their atmosphere if not their fabric, Elisabeth Beazley's chapter warns. Some insist that in a democratic society everyone has a right to easy access, with full interpretation, to any site. But popularity already severely restricts views of Stonehenge and now begins to threaten the ambience of Avebury as well. Soon no truly spectacular monument may be left for those who seek the past on their own terms, unobstructed by crowds or car parks or fences. It is already hard to find an American historical landmark neither obliterated by progress nor Disneyfied by popularity; to be saved for true appreciation, some sites need to be hidden, not advertised. As an Arkansas newspaper reported, 'no one knows where the historic Goose Creek Rock shelter is located, and the Washington Office of Archeology and Historic Preservation wants to keep it that way' (*New Yorker*, 4 December, 1978, p. 45).

It is equally hard to reconcile present-day entrepreneurial uses with any sense of heritage, for large-scale farming and manufacturing increasingly erode an enduring sense of locale. Yet to residents and visitors alike, stability, continuity, and cherished features from times past are not luxuries but basic constituents of life.

Finally, this book makes it clear that the interests of a small professional elite need to be reconciled with those of the general public. Notwithstanding their television image, archaeologists do not satisfy public demands for meaning and mystery in prehistory; Peter J. Fowler notes that scholars' zeal for knowledge is remote from popular interests in death and treasure. Hareven and Langenbach show how important are the familiar landmarks of people's own past lives, over and above structures of general historical significance or aesthetic acclaim. Beazley warns that the inherited past in cathedrals, castles, and country houses now has to cater for more numerous but less knowledgeable visitors. For antiques collectors, Bevis Hillier notes, anything that seems to be old takes on value simply because it is not of our time. But the personal and communal meanings that the public at large attach to the surviving past often involve forms of use and of interpretation which fly in the face of established canons of truth or beauty.

Coping with the contrived

All preservation alters the past, and hence makes it at least partly contrived; but new techniques of display increasingly refashion relics into modern artifacts. The past's new popularity spawns pseudo-historical scenes, some reconstructed from surviving shells, others built from scratch. On these 'historic' sites actors in period costumes bring history to life, re-enacting the shoeing of horses, the dipping of candles, the killing of desperadoes, the clangour of ancient battle. Such interpretative re-enactments, still most common in the United States, are no longer shunned even in Britain. A diorama with fanciful depictions of early armour introduces visitors to Battle Abbey, transforming 1066 into *1066 and All That*. At Blickling Hall, in Norfolk, National Trust re-enactments feature the Earl of Buckinghamshire in eighteenth-century costume and require the vicar in period garb to baptize the same village infant ten times a week.

Such operations do make history vivid for millions who would otherwise pass ancient monuments by with a blind or bored eye. But they are apt, in the process, to turn venerable places into self-conscious replicas of themselves, seeming to bear out gloomy prognostications that Britain may degenerate into a quaint museum of antiquities.

The prevalence of replicas and memorials also tends to relegate actual survivals to a back seat. A copy of Abraham Lincoln's restored log cabin birthplace is almost lost inside the modern marble Greek temple that houses it. Mark Twain's actual home in Hannibal, Missouri, attracts less attention than Tom Sawyer's. An old bar in a nineteenth-century building at Rockefeller Center in New York lost its lease to a nineteenth-century replica with a phony 'real old-fashioned nineteenth-century tavern', notes Huxtable (*Kicked a Building Lately?* p. 259). *Early American Decorating,* a popular magazine, advises readers that 'the essential flavor of Colonial is easy to capture' – for example, enlarged and tinted old photographs in suitably weathered frames 'give much the same impression as a genuine oil' (Winter 1979, p. 49). Hagerty's, an American repro-furniture firm that prides itself on historical respectability, nonetheless sells do-it-yourself staining for 'that 200-year-old look', and tells customers 'it is always flattering to have your creations mistaken for originals'. Some reproductions are avowedly *better* than originals: a manufacturer of a rustic log cabin boasts that 'Davy Crockett sure never had it so good!' – just as the copy of the Vieux Carré at Disneyland has been praised as *cleaner* than the original in New Orleans. Contrivers of new pasts follow the precept in James Dallaway's *Anecdotes of the Arts in England* (1800) that 'a happy imitation is of much more value than a defective original'.

History in books is no less contrived than on the ground. The Michigan Historical Society sells T-shirts with the legend 'History Tells It Like It Was'. But history often tells it how it *should* have been, if not how it should be now. As Frances FitzGerald shows in *America Revised* (1979), American history textbooks frequently imply that the national values they catalogue have not changed at all in three centuries.

Does preservation stifle creativity?

Preservation is a cause now embraced by millions. Saving old structures often costs less in materials, energy, and capital than replacing them with new buildings, and national pride or tourism may also justify their retention. But do these facts warrant preserving as much as we do? Owen Luder, now president of the Royal Institute of British Architects, thinks that 'much local authority rehabilitation of old housing represents poor value today and a large scale maintenance problem for the next generation' (*Building*, 15 December, 1978, p. 35).

Others charge that excessive admiration of old buildings inhibits contemporary creativity. Helping old buildings to survive pre-empts space and talent from new ones, in their view; the taste for the antique stifles innovation. Antiquities may exhaust too much of our energy, as Nathaniel Hawthorne thought at the British Museum as long ago as 1856. He admired the frieze of the Parthenon, the Elgin Marbles, Egyptian statues, but feared their stultifying effect, as he relates in his *English Notebooks* (p. 294):

The present is burthened too much with the past. We have not time, in our earthly existence, to appreciate what is warm with life, and immediately around us; yet we heap up all these old shells, out of which human life has long emerged, casting them off forever. I do not see how future ages are to stagger under all this dead weight, with the additions that will be continually made to it.

Much more of the past has since accumulated, yet we seem to welcome its weight, to regard the old rather than the new as 'warm with life'. 'Conservationists rob us of our cultural self-confidence', Douglas Johnson fears (*Vole*, 5, 1978, p. 43). 'We can no longer create, construct, imagine something new. We have to conserve, preserve, restore.'

Where the past is gone we replace it with pale ghosts intended mainly to 'fit in' with what has been preserved. Conservation-style architecture may be well-mannered and discreet, but it is often depressingly low-key. Many old buildings are preserved not just for their architectural merit but for fear of the bleak, blank, monolithic, brutal structures that would replace them. Some critics impute to preservationists the view that only past epochs produced authentic things. 'Beneath the visible attachment to "souvenirs", to photographs, memorabilia, old movies, old furniture, old styles in clothes,' writes Anthony Brandt (*Atlantic Monthly*, December 1970, p. 60), 'runs this sense that everything important is somewhere else, in another time.'

Were nostalgia confined to a few avid collectors of antiques, a few old grumblers, a few aspects of the built environment, it might be harmless enough, 'but for a whole culture to be looking backward is surely alarming'. Conservationists are said to 'wish to stop things happening; ... to prevent old buildings from being pulled down and new buildings from being put up,' Johnson adds, 'because they fear the future, they dislike the present, and they think things were better in the past'.

While such complaints caricature the preservation movement and exaggerate its impact, there is no gainsaying that they reflect anxiety about the implications of our intense attachment to the past. We are not the first generation to feel this way, to be sure. Edward Gibbon's *Decline and Fall* shows that a similar feeling of all good times lying behind, of uncreative adulation of things and persons past, infected the Roman Empire near its end. Second-century taste 'prostrated itself before Greek models, and educated

Romans grew ecstatic over ruins', Peter Gay puts it in *The Enlightenment* (1970, pp. 119-20). 'This indiscriminate antiquarian movement was not so much a cause as a symptom of exhaustion, of self contempt.' Like them, we are more apt to cling to inherited things than to emulate them.

By contrast, artists and architects from the Renaissance through the nineteenth century, harking back to Greece and Rome or to the Middle Ages, were excited by the *spirit* of ancient times as well as by their remains. They cared less about preserving the past than about using it as an inspiration for their own works. Historical visions drawn from books, from artifacts, from landscapes, inspired them not simply to revere but to rival antiquity. Some of their creations copied or imitated antique models, but most were freshly inspired by a freely reinterpreted past. Structures modelled after antique precepts embellished Europe and America: towns and cities, gardens, buildings, furnishings, paintings, sculpture recalled classical or Gothic forms and patterns. British preference for historically-derived themes and decor survived in vestigial form in Tudoresque and other revival semi-detached houses of the 1920s and 1930s. Indeed, a large part of what has been made or built in the past five centuries reflects this eclectic use of tradition.

Appreciation of the past today, however, means protecting ancient structures, not making new ones after their example. We save old buildings, but do not look to them for models. Survivals are hardly ever used as sources of contemporary inspiration. Scholarly knowledge about an increasing range of past epochs, styles, and forms expands partly at the expense of living involvement with any past. Indeed, a past so indiscriminately preserved is difficult to use creatively. Few architects deliberately employ antiquity; those who do use antique motifs in a humorous or ironic way, as if embarrassed to be caught admiring them – 'a classicism without class', as Charles Jencks puts it in 'Post-Modern Classicism' (*Architectural Design*, 5/6, 1980, p. 5).

The rejection of tradition as a source of creativity

28 Nineteenth-century use of the antique heritage: classical sculpture at Ny Carlsberg Glyptothek, Copenhagen

29 Twentieth-century use of the antique heritage: pop classical sign, Caesar's Palace, Las Vegas, Nevada

disjoins past from present, leaving what is preserved in a segregated realm of its own. Our cultural forebears made no such disjunction. Renaissance structures redolent of the past were often viewed as more truly antique than actual survivals. Neoclassical architects, painters, and patrons experienced the past as part of their present, imagining themselves in intimate converse with Greek or Roman poets and philosophers. What we make today may fit in with treasured survivals, but is seldom a dynamic reaffirmation of them. Many post-war architects came to feel the burden of the great buildings of the past, just as the great writers of the past – Shakespeare, Milton – weighed on eighteenth-century poets and playwrights, who were convinced that they could neither match nor imitate their legacy. 'The greatest single cultural problem we face', concludes W. J. Bate in *The Burden of the Past and the English Poet* (1971, p. 134), 'is how to use a heritage, when we know and admire so much about it.'

To prescribe or proscribe how to treat the past is pointless, for our view of it is determined by everything that we are and do. Yet to assess our own feelings against those of other times, to enter vicariously into our predecessors' modes of experiencing their pasts, can provide an illuminating historical perspective. We cannot emulate Dante in walking with Virgil, Petrarch in corresponding with Livy, or Holbach in enjoying conversing with Horace, or gaze on ruins as Shelley did, but we can appreciate the strength of these empathetic connections, and recognize that the pull of the past can lead in other directions than our own. We may question the authenticity of Renaissance and Enlightenment rapport with their beloved Ancients, but we cannot deny that antiquity truly inspired them. We may be spared the ubiquitous Irish sense of past grievances, but we can admire the imaginative force with which Irish storytellers, memories, and landmarks bring the past to life. We may find Victorian obsessions with Anglo-Saxon origins no less *outré* than some scholars today find the anachronisms of Alex Haley's *Roots*, but we can envy the

231

nineteenth century's capacity to draw communal sustenance from historical paintings, architecture, and literature.

Once we become alert to other routes to the past, we may see our own relations with it as less binding, more contingent on circumstances, and destined some day to give way to other forms of appreciation. Our grandchildren may wonder no less at our passion for authentically restored old buildings than we smile at the naiveté of our grandparents, who thought that visiting a site where a hero fought – or even slept – would improve one's character and inspire patriotism.

Awareness of the myriad ways in which others have appreciated their heritage could enlarge our tolerance for present-day manipulations of the past that often seem false or bizarre. Even a sanitized, Disneyfied past has its virtues; Ye Olde Englishing, mock Georgian, and instant mansards are popular partly because they convey a more lively and up-to-date impression of things past than do scrupulously maintained genuine survivals. Better a misguided awareness of history than none, a lighthearted dalliance with the past than a wholesale rejection of it. So too with copies of sham pasts; forgery is in a sense the sincerest form of flattery.

Restorations and reconstructions need not always strive to be wholly 'correct'; things can be enjoyed as 'old' even though patently inauthentic. Our heritage does not continually demand solemn respect; the past can be amusing as well as serious, incongruous as well as meaningful. We can afford to smile at the anachronisms that make bygone times seem like those old *Punch* cartoons to which new legends are fitted. The past is often funny because it *is* old hat. The very notion of preservation is so artificial that it invites mockery at its extravagances – the three heads of John the Baptist reverentially preserved in different churches; the twelve foreskins of Christ; fragments of the True Cross enough to build a galleon; the recent news that the viscera of Henry V, which released an authentically unpleasant smell on being unearthed in a pot in France, have rejoined His Majesty's remains in Westminster Abbey;

30 The reconstructed past: Iron Age huts at Lejre Research Centre, Denmark

31 The emblematic past: thatched and half-timbered vehicle at Fordingbridge, Hampshire, *c.* 1972

the two birthplaces of President Lyndon Johnson, one an 'authentic' reconstruction of the actual birthplace, the other a cabin erected by Johnson himself as the birthplace he would like to have had. Eighteenth-century ruins and follies, now doubly ruined by time and disuse, divert as well as instruct us.

Revival buildings are nowadays often scorned for being either untrue to their prototypes or mere copies of them. But revivals always reflect the genius of their own epoch as well as that of the valued past. Artists should never be afraid of their work appearing derivative and unoriginal, as James Lees-Milne writes in *Ancestral Voices* (1975, p. 40), 'for whatever they produce inevitably retains the flavour of their own epoch'.

Very little of what has endured, on the other hand, can be certified as original. Our apprehension of any past derives only in small measure from its own remains, much more from subsequent copies and emulations. The current image of 'classical', for example, depends far less on actual Greek and Roman relics than on Hellenistic, humanistic, and neoclassicist versions. Much of North America bears a classical face of the nineteenth and twentieth centuries.

We need not save everything old in order to appreciate the tangible past. Indeed, we cannot do so: more of every epoch has perished than has survived, and most of what remains is fragile and doomed. The past is not only the Rock of Ages; it is also the passing moment, and transience lends the past its own special charms.

A few emblematic elements may suffice to convey historical continuity; mere fragments of the past can lend temporal weight to a new creation. Thus the renovated eighteenth-century dome lends Boston's restored Quincy Market an aura of antiquity, its freshly minted classicism juxtaposed against the worn, ornate lettering of a few nineteenth-century shopkeepers' signs in a twentieth-century mercantile setting; the past is here preserved not in fabric or texture, but in emblem and insignia.

Similarly at South Salem, New York, a new church

replaces the eighteenth-century meeting-house which burned down in 1971; at first glance a replica of the old, it is in fact only reminiscent of it, streamlining or jettisoning the original forms and decorative elements, its steeple setbacks muted and clad with aluminium siding. Inside, the church is wholly transformed; the focus is no longer at the end of the nave but to one side, towards which all the pews informally front. Decor and fittings are entirely new, save for the cross, the pulpit, and a wall ornament of gnarled wood, suggestive of the old church through their look of age. Behind the new altar a picture window opens onto the old burying ground, gravestones offering an intriguing glimpse of the past from the pews. At some historical attractions, modern visitor centres are carefully screened from view. But shutting out the present is not the best way to achieve or sustain a sense of continuity. Contemporary features, deliberately inserted into otherwise mummified historic precincts, give point to the past in many locales.

A past appreciated only by means of preservation satisfies mainly passive needs. A heritage should move its admirers to participate, not merely to look on; in order to incorporate surviving relics into our own lives, we must make something new of them, acting on what we venerate. The past is not simply a film flashing us back to earlier, more compelling times; it is a theatre of real life, from which present-day actors draw creative sustenance. A present that is content simply with retrospection can build no past worthy of the future.

Let me summarize my conclusions.

What to save. We should save more than we might like to, remembering the pace of destruction and the needs of posterity. Future generations will require relics that we have touched lightly or not at all. But as we can save nothing for ever, we should keep a balance between public symbols and fields of care, great monuments of all time and intimate familiar scenes of our own immediate past.

How to use what we save. Not everything old belongs in

museums or historic precincts; most of what is saved should be a vital part of the present, but tangible heritage cannot be wholly adapted to modern needs; nor would we like it if it did.

Coping with the contrived. The past is what we make it, not only what it was; the process of preservation changes the look and feel, if not the form and substance, of protected sites and artifacts. We must accept many such transformations as inevitable. We may value what is authentic, but most relics we live with have been – have to have been – adapted, transformed, modernized.

The past as inspiration. We do not preserve too much but do too little besides; we could treat our heritage more creatively. Past and present should often be commingled, not separated. Every trace we inherit is a testament not only to the spirit of the past but to our present perspectives.

Even those who deny their past need contact and continuity with antiquity; rejecting tradition may simply reflect a demeaning or inadequate history. The great majority may 'not give a damn about the past', as Fowler says here, but their ignorance does not vitiate their need of it. Our views of the past also change as we ourselves move through time. Even if a rebellious youngster now takes no interest in his past, it must be secured for him, for he will finally become an old fogey. The past belongs to everyone: the need to return home, to recall the view, to refresh a memory, to retrace a heritage, is universal and essential.

FURTHER READING

Bate, Walter Jackson. *The Burden of the Past and the English Poet*. London: Chatto & Windus, 1971. How eighteenth-century English writers coped with the crippling effects of their profound admiration for their literary forebears, whose achievements they felt unable to equal.

Binney, Marcus, and others. *Satanic Mills: Industrial Architecture in the Pennines*. London: SAVE Britain's Heritage [1978]. The case for preserving the textile mills of Lancashire and Yorkshire, among the grandest buildings of the Industrial Revolution.

Brett, Lionel. *Parameters and Images: Architecture in a Crowded World.* London: Weidenfeld and Nicolson, 1970. An eminent architect's statement of faith.

Clark, Kenneth. *The Gothic Revival: An Essay in the History of Taste.* London: Constable, 1928; 3rd edition, John Murray, 1962; paperback, 1978. Classic account of the transition from romantic to ecclesiological appreciation and use of medieval architectural styles and motifs.

Ely, David. *Time Out.* London: Secker & Warburg, 1968. A fictional historian's reaction to attempts to restore Britain in its entirety, including all the relics of its past, precisely as it would have been but for a catastrophic nuclear mishap.

FitzGerald, Frances. *America Revised: History Schoolbooks in the Twentieth Century.* Boston: Atlantic–Little Brown, 1979; paperback, Random House/Vintage, 1980. Shows how textbook writers and publishers have continually reinterpreted the American past to suit the perspectives – and the marketplace – of the moment.

Hawthorne, Nathaniel. *The English Notebooks.* New York: Modern Language Association, 1941. The great New England novelist, who was American consul in Liverpool in the 1850s, reveals his ambivalence to relics of the past, alike an oppressive burden that crippled initiative, and an essential attribute of a creative environment. The conflict between the good and the evil past, a commonplace in mid-nineteenth-century America, is central to Hawthorne's *The House of the Seven Gables.*

Huxtable, Ada Louise. *Kicked a Building Lately?* New York: New York Times, 1976; Quadrangle Books, 1978. Articles about the demolition, alteration, and preservation of various historic buildings in the United States, by the doyenne of American architectural critics.

Lees-Milne, James. *Ancestral Voices.* London: Chatto & Windus, 1975. Fascinating account of the author's visits to historic English country houses during the 1940s with a view to their acquisition by the National Trust.

Meyer, Karl. *The Plundered Past: The Traffic in Art Treasures.* New York: Atheneum, 1973; London: Hamish Hamilton, 1974. A graphic review of the plunder of archaeological sites for sale to museums and collectors, and the attendant loss to our knowledge of the past.

Tuan, Yi-Fu. 'Space and Place: Humanistic Perspective', in *Progress in Geography,* Vol. 6 (London: Edward Arnold, 1974), pp. 211-52. The values found in familiar and symbolic artifacts and locales, amplified in Tuan's subsequent *Space and Place: The Perspective of Experience* (Minneapolis: University of Minnesota Press, 1977).

Notes on Contributors

Elisabeth Beazley is an architect and author who works as a consultant planner chiefly on matters concerning the conservation of historic buildings and their surroundings, in relation to problems created by the pressure of tourism. She has written *The Countryside on View* (1971); *Designed for Recreation* (1969); *Madocks and the Wonder of Wales* (1967); *A Shell Guide to North Wales* (with Lionel Brett, 1971); *Collins' Companion Guides to North and South Wales* (with Peter Howell, 1975 and 1977). She has worked in Iran on various projects and is engaged in a study of vernacular buildings on the Iranian plateau, particularly those designed to withstand severe desert conditions, which will appear as *Living with the Desert* (with Michael Harverson), to be published by Aris and Phillips, Warminster.

Marcus Binney is architectural editor of *Country Life*, chairman of SAVE Britain's Heritage, was Secretary of the UK Committee of the International Council on Monuments and sites from 1972 to 1981. He is the editor and joint author of numerous books, including *Preservation Pays* (1978); *Satanic Mills: Industrial Architecture in the Pennines* (1978); *Change and Decay: The Future of Our Churches* (1977); *Chapels and Churches; Who Cares?* (1977); and *The Destruction of the Country House 1875-1975* (1974). He was a member of the Working Party chaired by Lord Montagu of Beaulieu which produced *Britain's Historic Buildings: A Policy for Their Future Use* (1980).

Peter J.Fowler was for six years at the Salisbury office of the Royal Commission on Historical Monuments (England) before moving to Bristol University in 1965, where he became Reader in Archaeology in 1973. He returned to the Royal Commission as Secretary in 1979. His interests include landscape archaeology, agrarian history, conservation and the popularization of archaeology. He is the author of *Wessex* (1967), *Approaches to Archaeology* (1977), and 'Later Prehistory' in the *Cambridge Agrarian History of England and Wales*, Vol. I (1981); editor of *Archaeology and the Landscape* (1972) and *Recent Work in Rural Archaeology* (1975); and joint editor of *The Roman West Country* (1976) and *Early Land Allotment in the British Isles* (1978). He has also served as Honorary Secretary for the Council for British Archaeology and Vice-President of the Prehistoric Society.

Max Hanna has been manager of socio-economic research for the English Tourist Board since 1975. He is the author of *Preservation Pays*

Notes on Contributors

(1978, with Marcus Binney); *English Cathedrals and Tourism* (1979); *English Heritage Monitor* (annual, 1977 to date). A member of the Georgian Group and the National Trust, and a Committee member of the Cobham Conservation Group, Max Hanna is currently continuing to work on the economic benefits generated by conservation.

Tamara K. Hareven is professor of history at Clark University, and research associate at the Center for Population Studies at Harvard. The author of *Eleanor Roosevelt: An American Conscience* (1968) and, with Randolph Langenbach, of *Amoskeag: Life and Work in an American Factory City* (1978), she has edited *Family and Kin in American Urban Communities* (1977), *Themes in the History of the Family* (1978) and *Transitions: The Family and the Life Course in Historical Perspective* (1978), and has co-edited several other books on childhood and the family. She is founder and editor of *The Journal of Family History*. Her *Family and Industrial Time* (Cambridge University Press) will appear in 1982.

Bevis Hillier, formerly Editor of the *Connoisseur,* Sales Room Correspondent and Antiques Correspondent of *The Times,* is the author of twenty books on art and antiques, including *Master Potters of the Industrial Revolution* (1965), *Pottery and Porcelain 1700-1914* (1968), *Art Deco of the 1920s and 30s* (1968), *Posters* (1969), *Austerity/Binge* (1975) and *The New Antiques* (1977). He is Chairman of the Thirties Society, which aims to preserve the best architecture of the 1920s and 30s. He is currently working on the authorized biography of Sir John Betjeman.

Michael Hunter is a Lecturer in History at Birkbeck College, University of London; his scholarly works include *John Aubrey and the Realm of Learning* (1975) and *Science and Society in Restoration England* (1981). He is also actively involved in local conservation in London, and has recently written a book on *The Victorian Villas of Hackney* for the Hackney Society.

Randolph Langenbach is a designer, architectural historian and photographer, who has pioneered in the preservation of industrial communities in New England and in England. He is the author of *A Future from the Past* (1977); *Amoskeag: Life and Work in an American Factory City* (with Tamara Hareven, 1978); and (with others) *Satanic Mills: Industrial Architecture in the Pennines* (SAVE Britain's Heritage, 1978), which accompanied an exhibition of his photographs shown in London and in Bradford in 1980.

David Lowenthal has been professor of geography at University College London since 1972. Prior to that he was research associate and Secretary of the American Geographical Society in New York, taught at several American universities, and did extensive research in the Caribbean. His interest in preservation stems from his biography of the nineteenth-century American pioneer conservationist, *George Perkins Marsh: Versatile Vermonter* (1958), whose 1864 classic *Man and Nature* Lowenthal also edited (1965). Studies of landscape tastes and environmental perception led to a concern with how the past is used and changed, of which this book is one outcome. His general study on the subject, *The Past Is Another Country* (Cambridge University Press), will appear in 1982.

John Popham is a chartered surveyor who has specialized in the conservation of buildings and landscapes. He is Director of the Suffolk Preservation Society and Secretary of the Suffolk Building Preservation Trust.

Ken Powell is an architectural historian and conservationist who lives in Leeds, where he works as Northern Secretary of the conservation group SAVE Britain's Heritage. He is currently writing a book on conserving the industrial town.

Hugh Prince is a Reader in Geography at University College London and the Editor of the *Journal of Historical Geography*. Among his publications are *Parks in England* (Shalfleet: Pinhorns, 1967), studies in historical geography in J. T. Coppock and H. C. Prince (eds), *Greater London* (1964), and articles on landscape tastes written jointly with David Lowenthal. He is now investigating changing attitudes towards historic buildings and ancient monuments in England. His study traces the histories of preservation, restoration and revival from 1500 to the present.

Matthew Saunders served briefly as a sub-editor of *Whitaker's Almanack*, before becoming Secretary of SAVE Britain's Heritage. For the past five years he has worked for the Ancient Monuments Society, latterly as its Secretary. A regular contributor to *Whitaker's Almanack* since 1976, he is the author of *The Buildings of Tottenham* (1979) and a contributor to Marcus Binney and David Pearce's *Railway Architecture* (1979). He is currently writing books on the Victorian architect S. S. Teulon and on the architecture of banks.

Sylvia Sayer was brought up on Dartmoor. Lady Sayer's great-grandfather Charles Burnard and grandfather (Robert) were founders of the Dartmoor Preservation Association in 1883, of which she herself was Chairman from 1951 to 1973 and is now Patron jointly with her husband. They live in an ancient farm house in Widecombe-in-the Moor and are Dartmoor commoners, with rights of grazing and turbary over extensive areas of the Moor. Lady Sayer has served as both parish and district councillor for Widecombe, and in 1952 became a member of Devon County Council's Dartmoor National Park Committee, from which she resigned in 1956 in protest against the prodigal allocation of land on southern Dartmoor for china clay working. She is a member of the Commons Preservation Society, the Council for National Parks, and the National Trust, and is a Vice-President of the Ramblers' Association.

Marion Shoard is a freelance writer on countryside matters. She worked on pest control for the Agricultural Research Council before deciding to devote her energies to countryside conservation. She joined the Council for the Protection of Rural England as assistant secretary with responsibility for planning and conservation. After four years at CPRE she left to research and write her book *The Theft of the Countryside* (1980).

Index